Red Line
Green Line
ticket

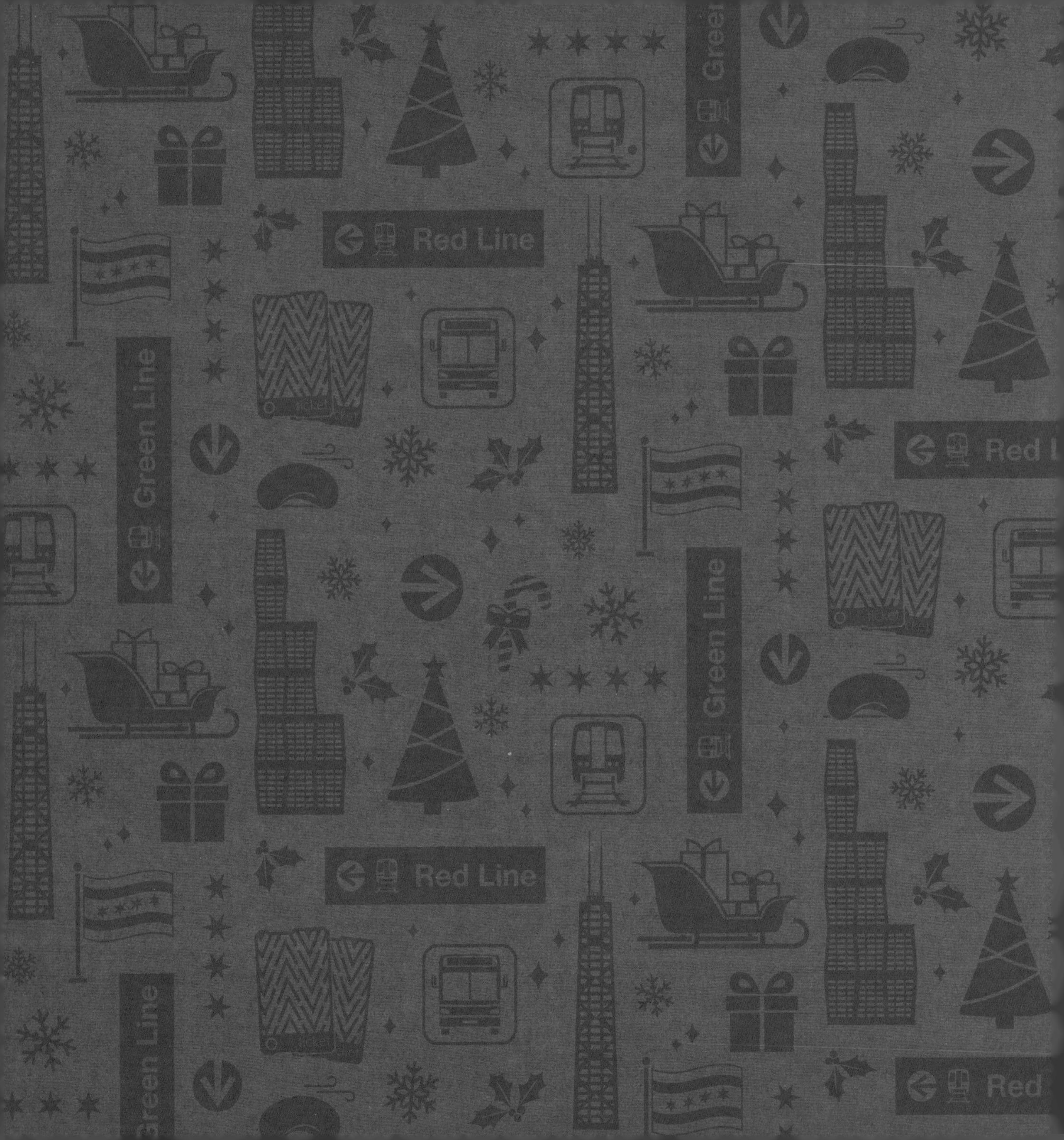
Red Line
Green Line

TROPE
PUBLISHING
Co.

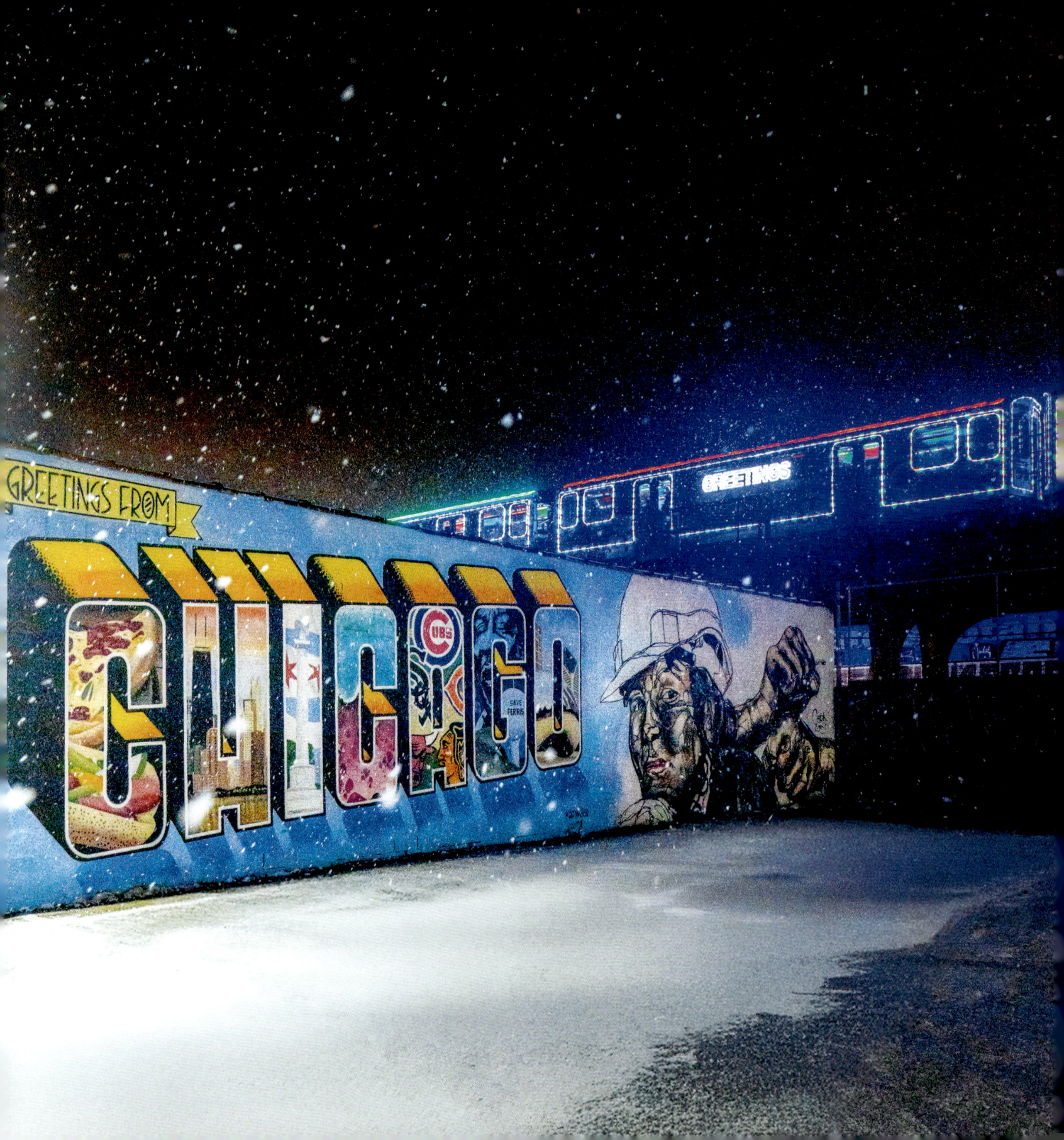
GREETINGS FROM
CHICAGO
SAVE FERRIS
GREETINGS

CHICAGO'S HOLIDAY TRAIN

DANIEL MORENO

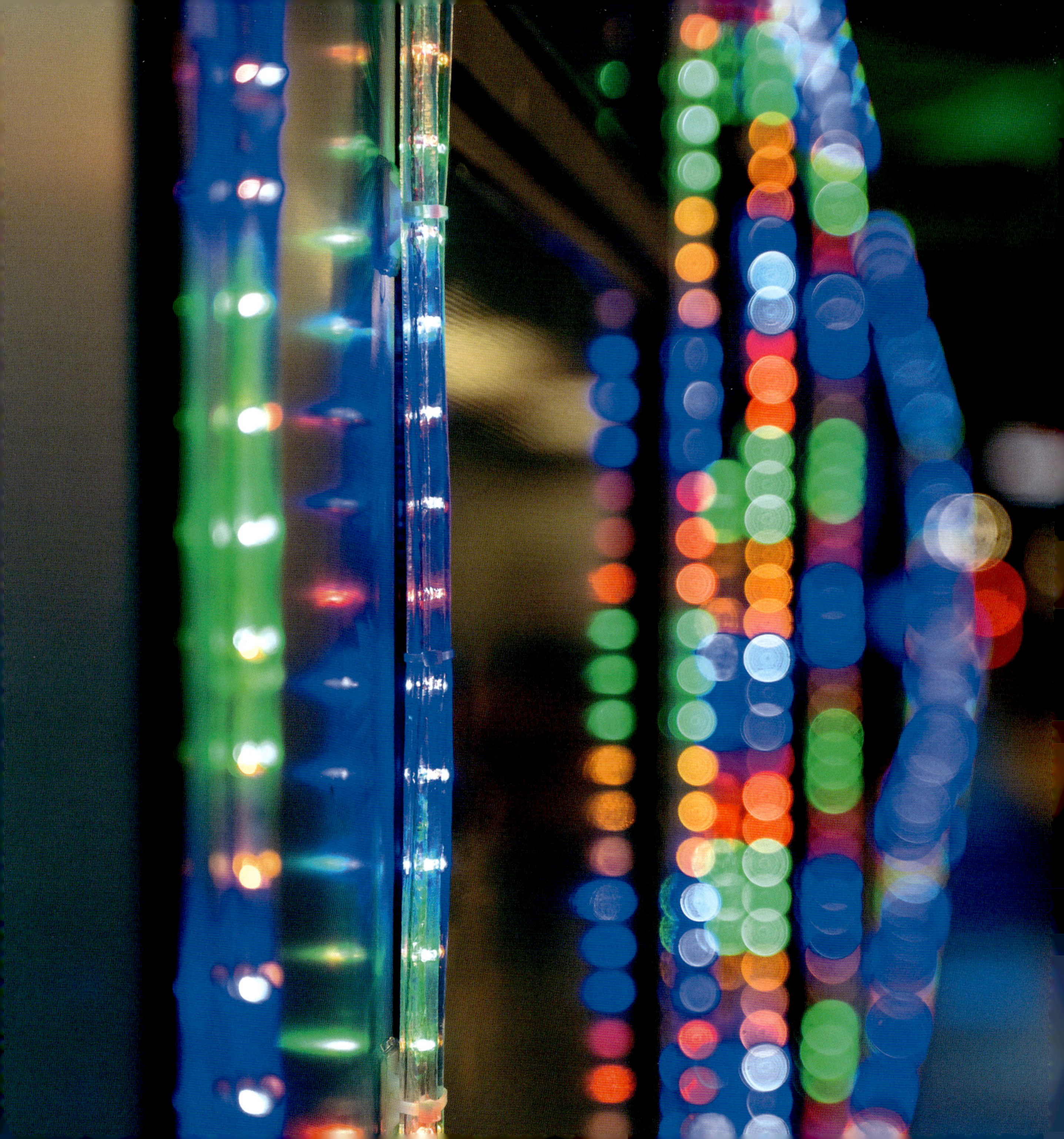

INTRODUCTION

Winter in Chicago arrives with biting winds, dry air, and fleeting daylight. Yet, amid the harshness of the season, there's a moment I always anticipate: the arrival of the Holiday Train, a bright and fleeting spectacle that never fails to lift my spirits. Ever since I moved to Chicago, the train has been a part of my daily life. Riding the train every day has made it feel like more than just a means of transportation; it has become a familiar presence, a thread woven into my experience of the city.

Chicago is a city that constantly offers captivating scenes for photography, and the train is an essential part of the city's landscape. But the Holiday Train's brief appearance during the Christmas season, lasting only a few weeks, makes it all the more special. Decked out in twinkling lights and bursting with festive cheer, it cuts through the city's gray winter days. It brings color and warmth wherever it goes. To me, the Holiday Train is more than a seasonal spectacle, it's a train of light. And photography, at its core, is the art of capturing light. The train's glow against the dark, snowy streets makes it an irresistible subject for photography. The contrast between its vibrant decorations and the muted tones of winter transforms each scene into something almost surreal.

As a photographer, I have spent years chasing Chicago's Holiday Train all around the city, trying to capture not just the vibrant colors and dazzling displays, but the emotions they stir and how it interacts with Chicago's landscape. In my pursuit, I have discovered countless corners of the city I might have otherwise overlooked. I've seen tired commuters break into unexpected smiles, and I've felt the collective joy of strangers momentarily united by a shared sense of awe.

This book is more than a collection of images; it is a personal journey through my passion for the Holiday Train and the way it transforms Chicago, even if just for a season. Whether you've ridden it countless times or are discovering it here for the first time, I hope these photographs bring you the same warmth, joy, and nostalgia they brought me while capturing them, because, in the end, the train doesn't just bring light to the city, it makes winter feel a little less harsh.

DANIEL MORENO

ABOUT THE

HOLIDAY TRAIN

The Chicago Transit Authority's Holiday Train began in 1992 when an out-of-service Blue Line train was being used to deliver food donations to charities across the city. The train sported a simple sign reading, "Season's Greetings from the CTA!"

Since those humble beginnings, the Holiday Train has grown into a Chicago tradition, expanding to run on all eight of the CTA's rail lines, covering over 200 miles of tracks, beginning in late November and running through late December each year. Decked out in multi-colored lights, red bows, candy cane pole wraps, and colored garlands, the Holiday Train brings a festive touch to everyone who rides it. Each six-car train features a custom exterior wrap that features new holiday and seasonal graphics each year; the wraps have been designed in-house by the CTA since 1998. In 2014, the Holiday Bus was added and now runs on 17 routes across the city.

The real highlight of the Holiday Train is Santa himself, who can be seen riding on open-air flatcars along with his reindeer and holiday trees, waving to passersby. A foot heater and warming hand bar behind the sleigh help keep Santa warm through rain, snow, and Chicago's frigid temperatures. He is even available for photo opportunities on certain days.

Over the years, there have been talks about discontinuing the Holiday Train, including in 2004 amidst a budget deficit and pending layoffs and again in 2020 during the COVID-19 pandemic, when the train ran without passengers. But the Holiday Train's fervent fans fought back, and the CTA Holiday Train remains a treasured tradition that Chicago residents—adults and children alike—look forward to each year.

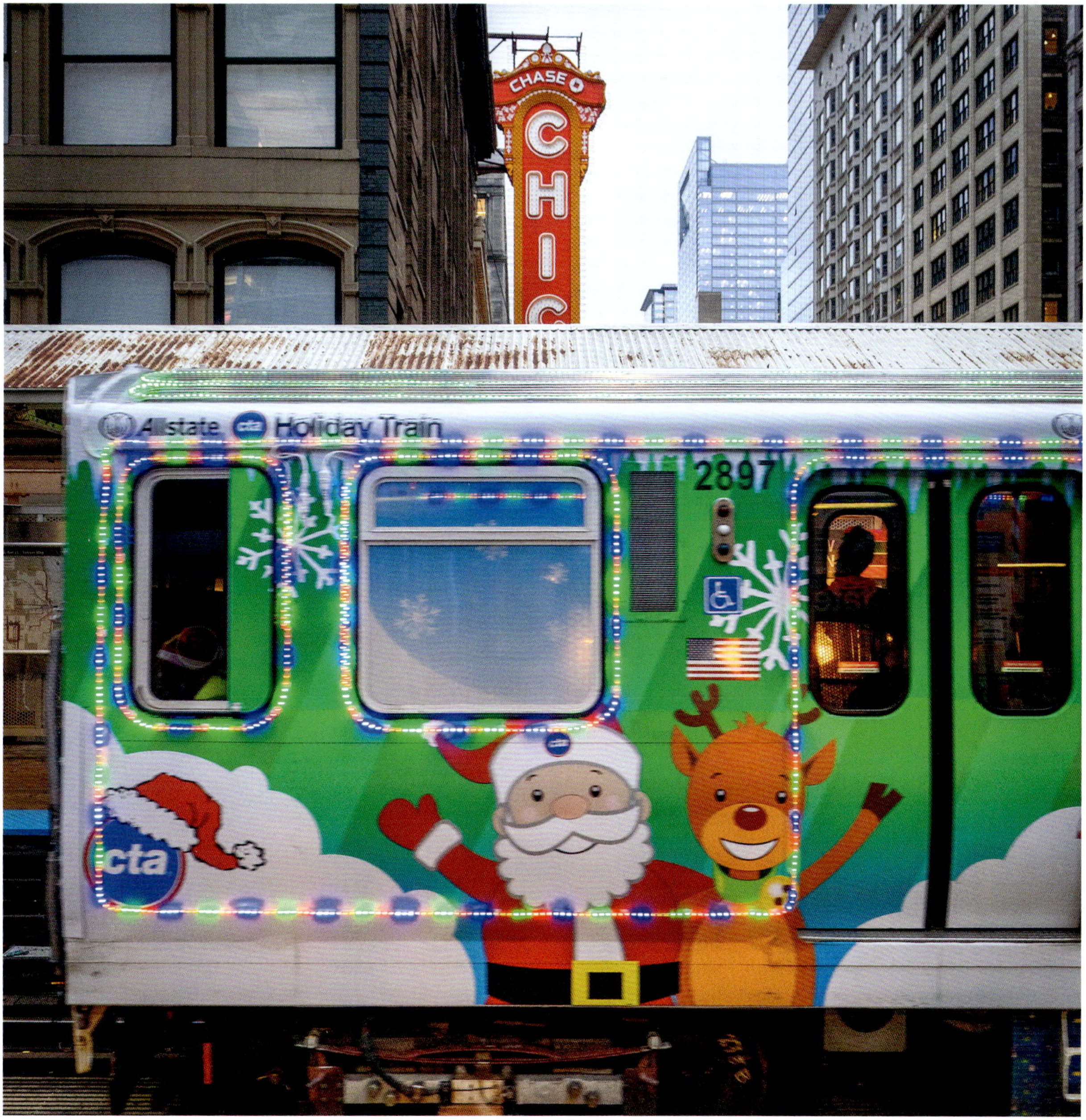

State and Lake CTA station

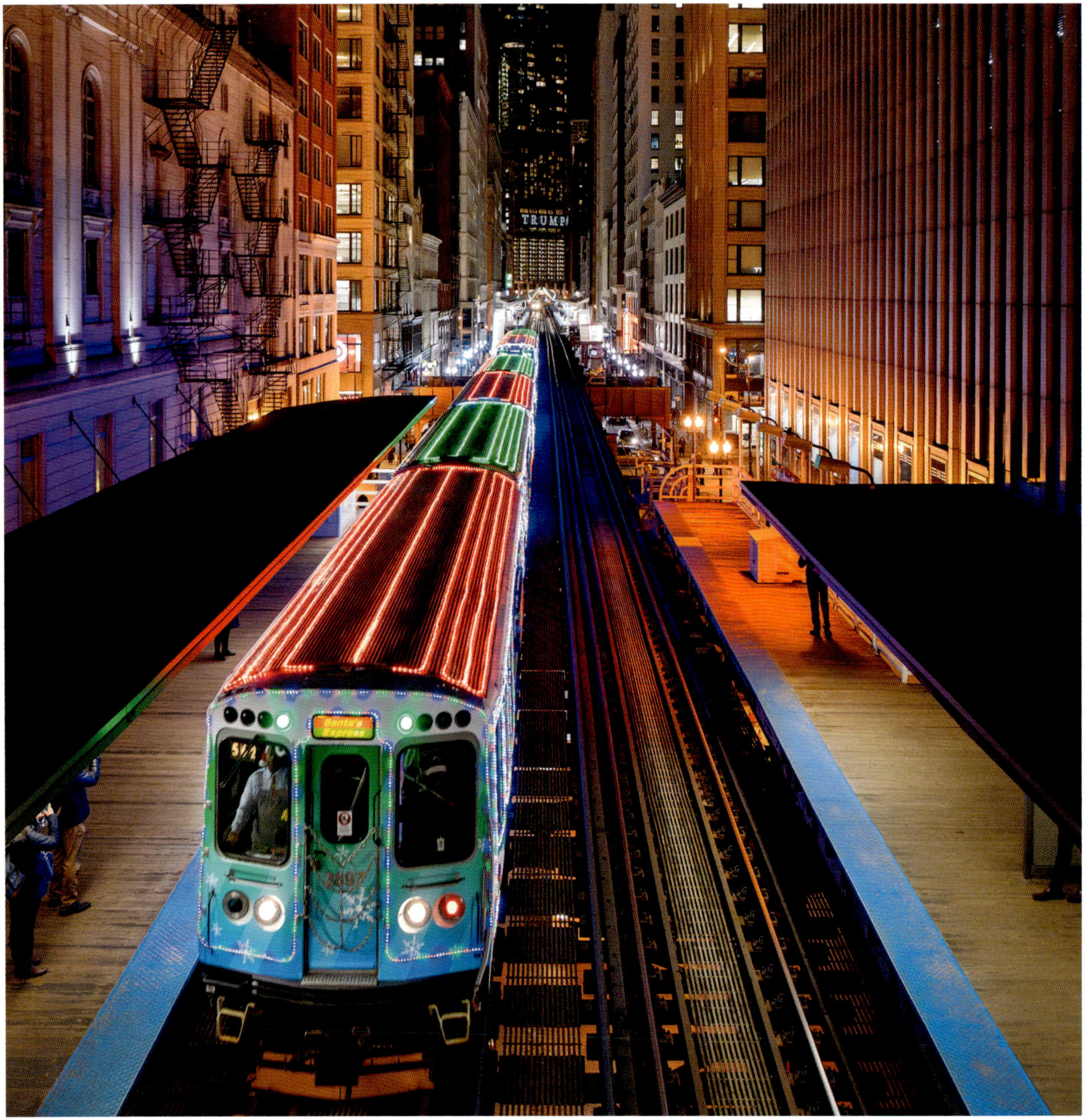

Looking down South Wabash Avenue

"The Allstate CTA Holiday Train and Bus are more than festive decorations—they are a unique Chicago holiday tradition that celebrates the goodwill of this city, and the hard work of CTA employees who are committed to making everyone's holidays a little brighter."

Former CTA President Dorval R. Carter, Jr.

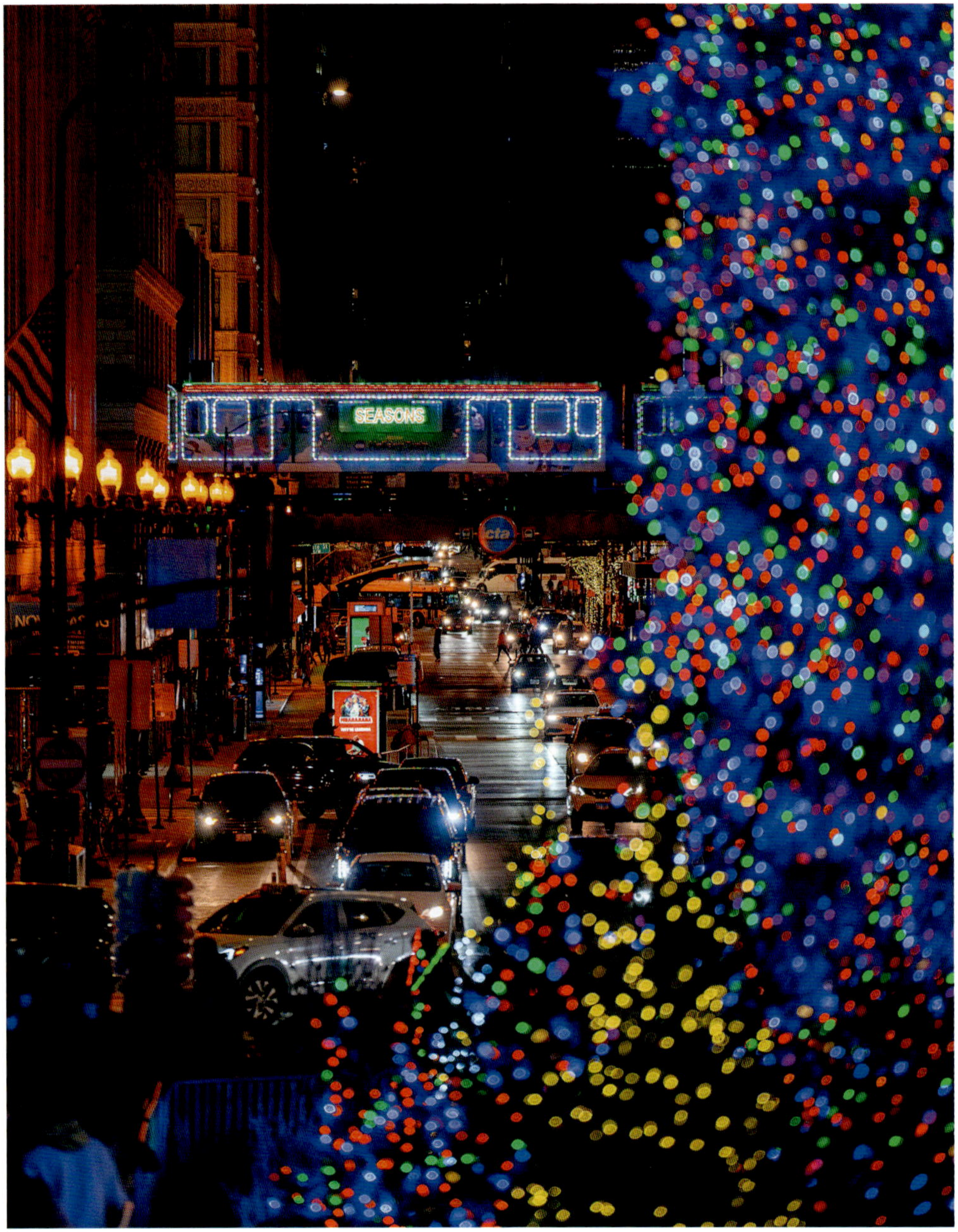

ABOVE: Looking west down East Washington Street **RIGHT:** Looking east down East Washington Street

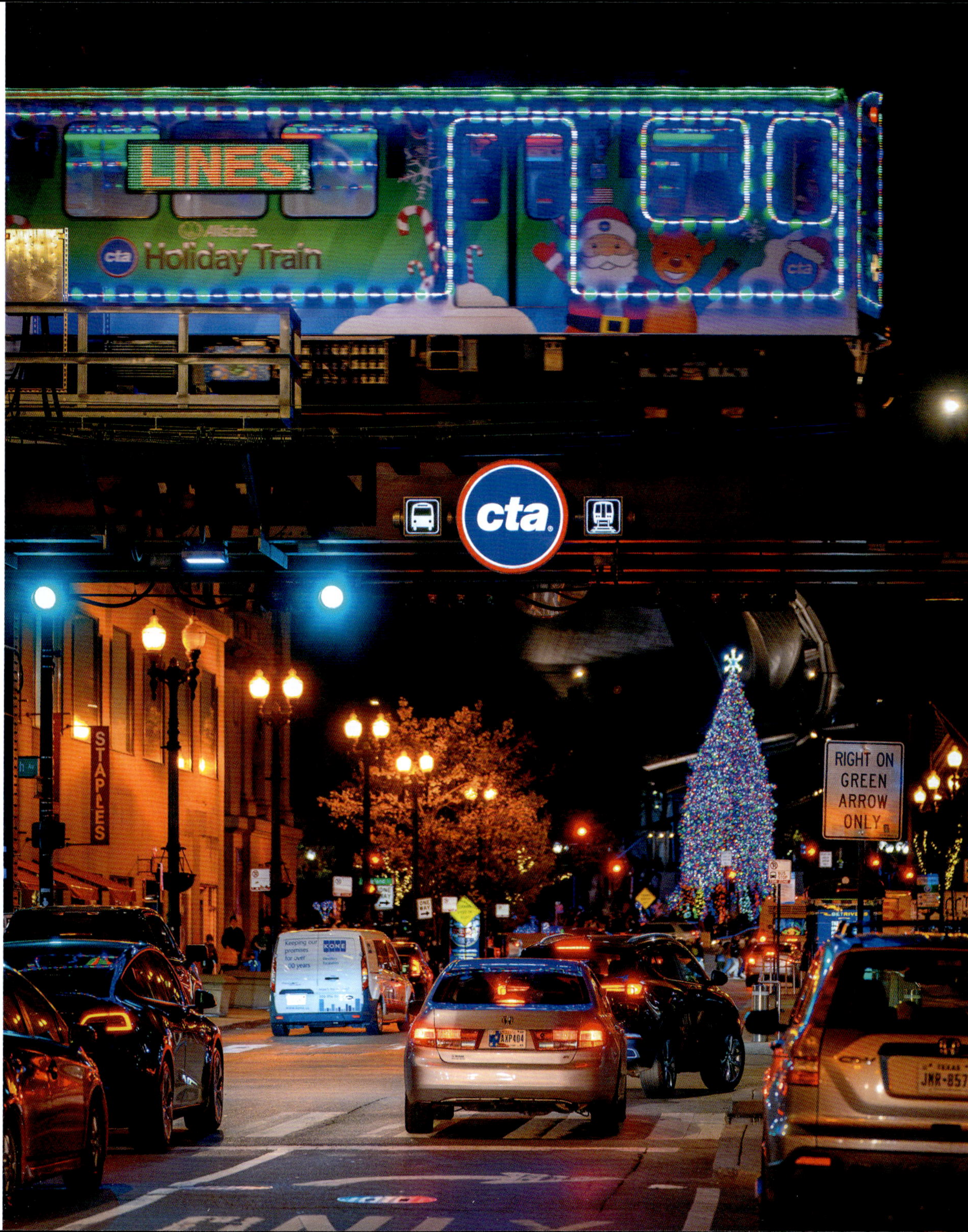

LINES
Allstate
cta Holiday Train
cta
STAPLES
RIGHT ON GREEN ARROW ONLY

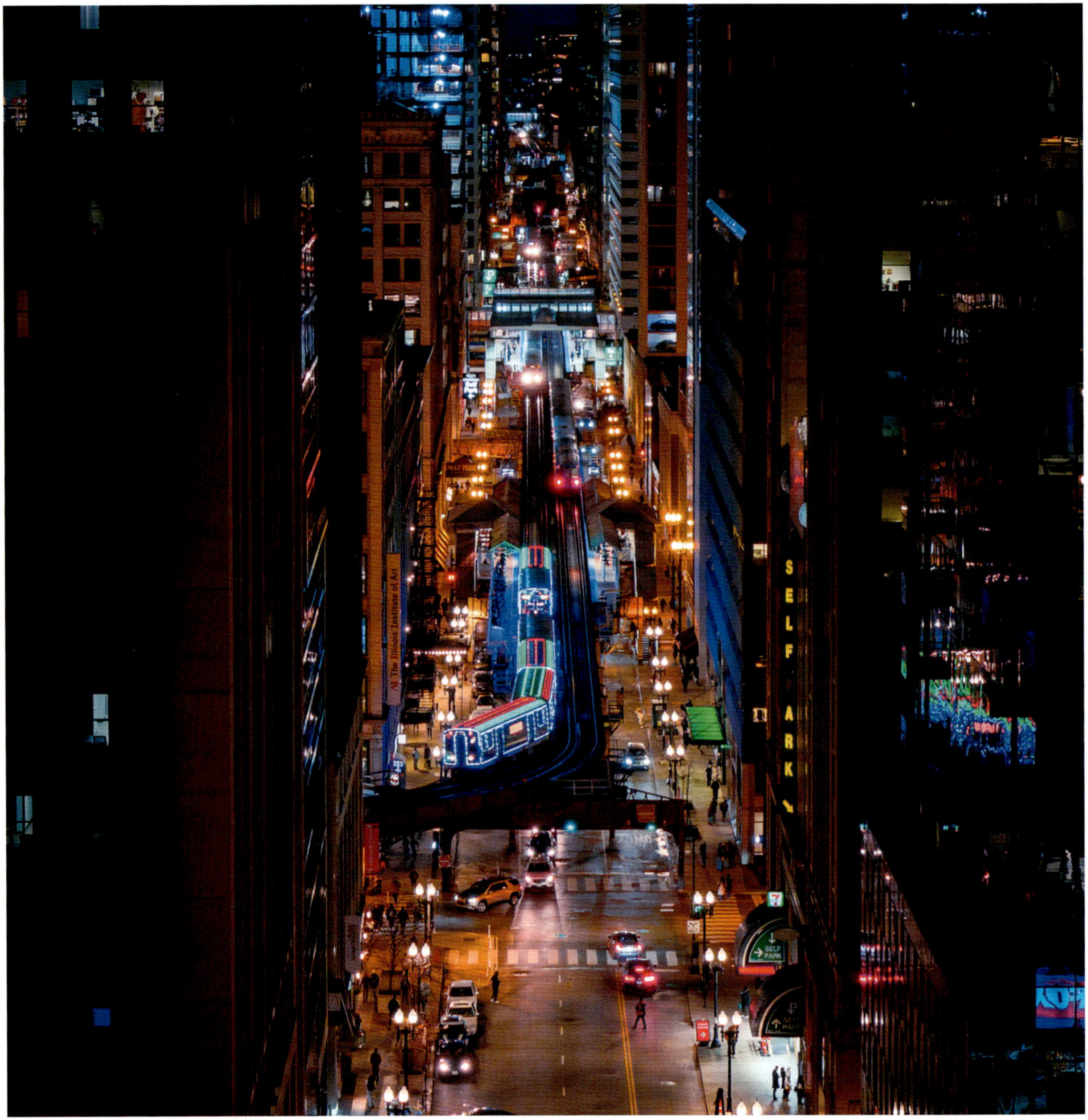

Above East Lake Street at State Street

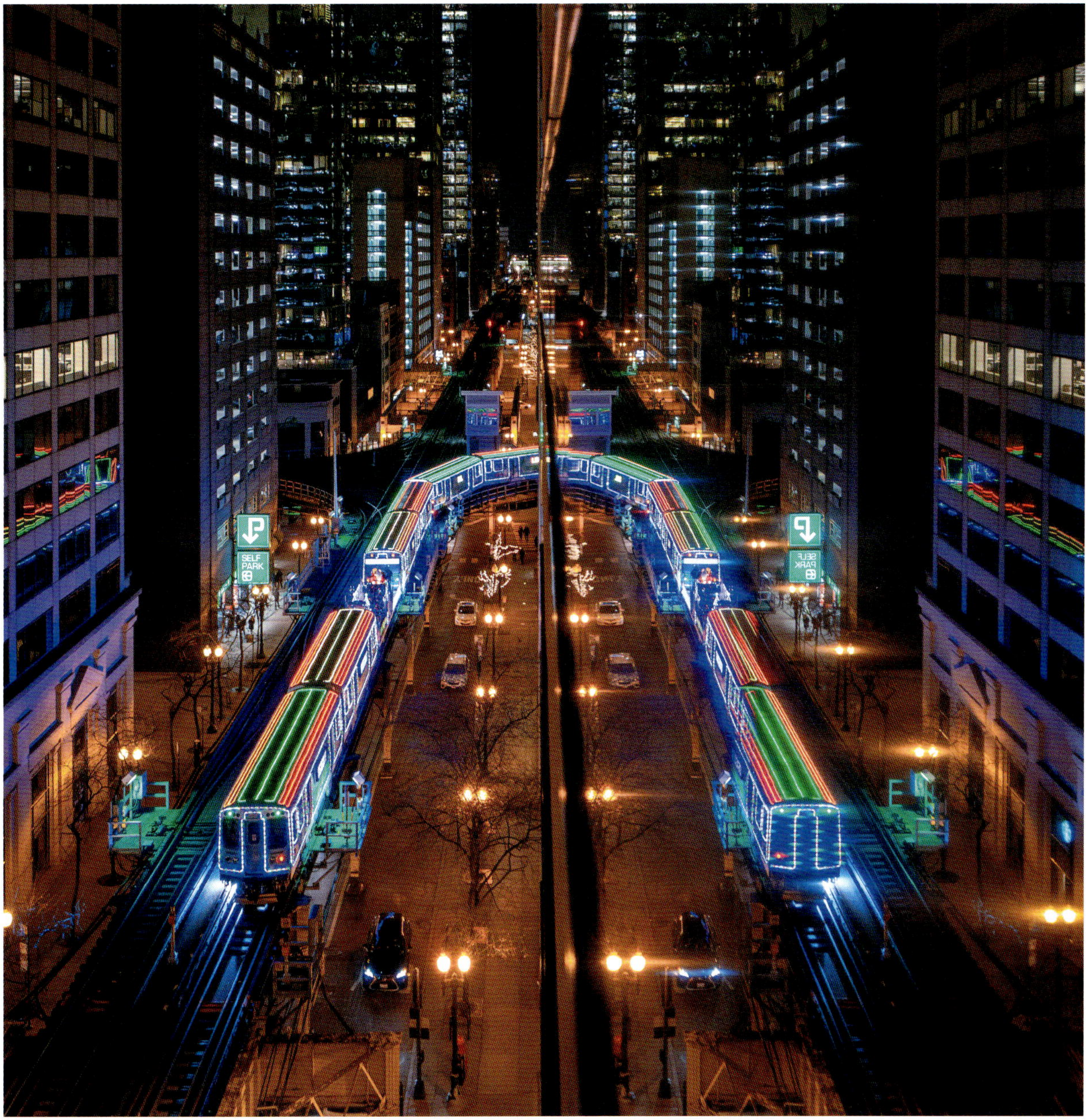

Above East Lake Street at Clark Street

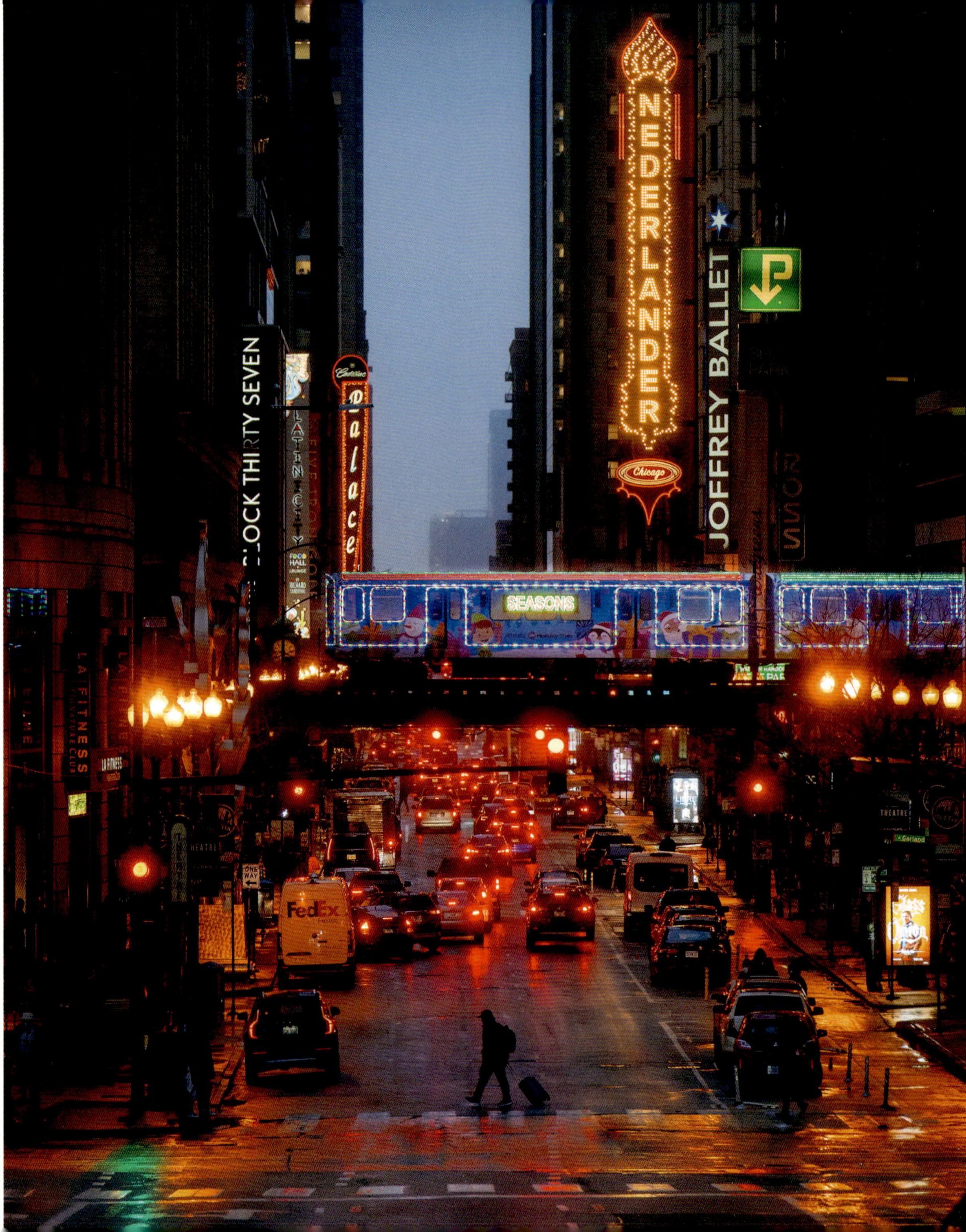
NEDERLANDER
Chicago
JOFFREY BALLET
BLOCK THIRTY SEVEN
LATIN CITY
Palace
SEASONS
LA FITNESS
FedEx

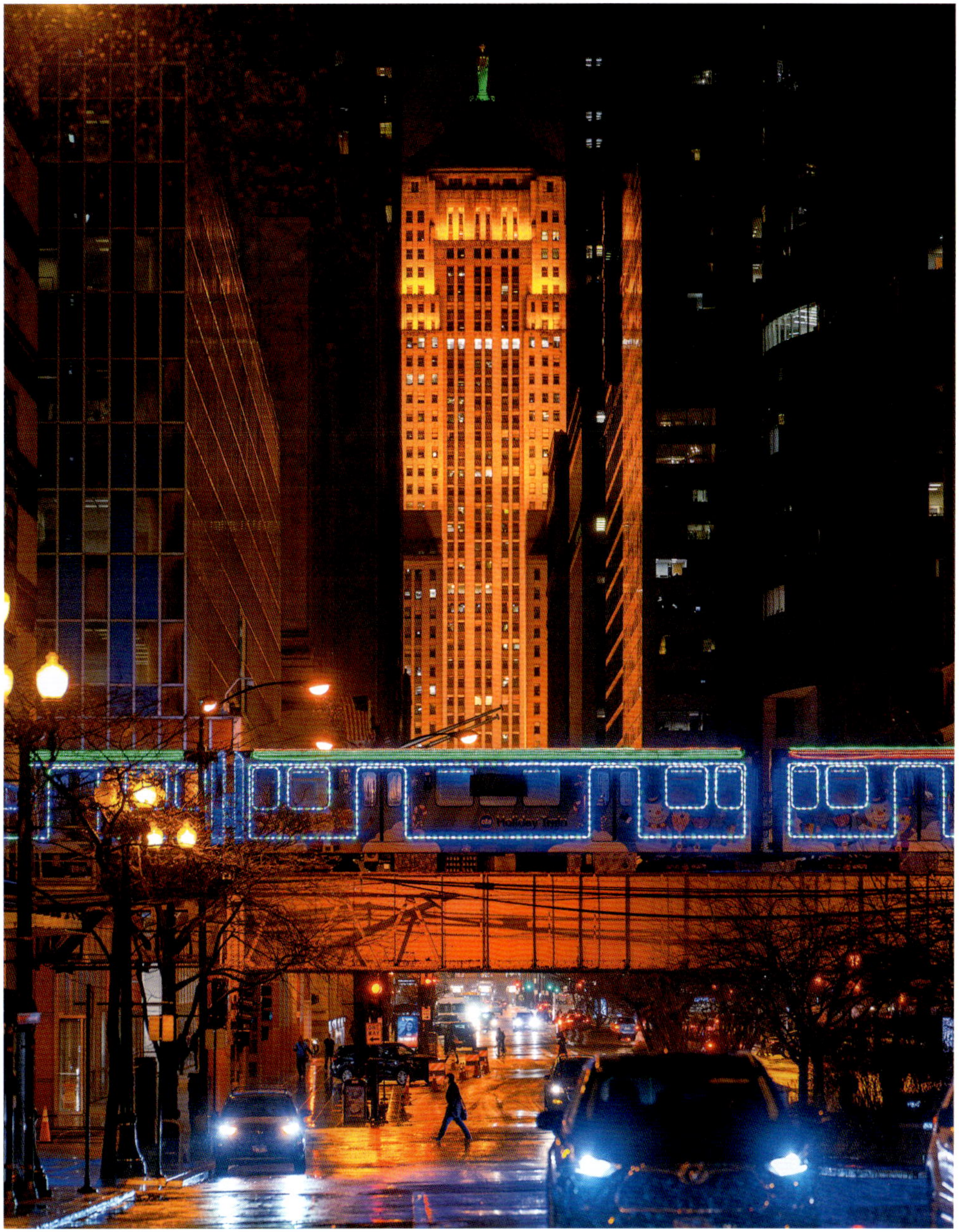

LEFT: Looking down East Randolph Street **ABOVE:** Looking down North LaSalle Street at the Chicago Board of Trade Building

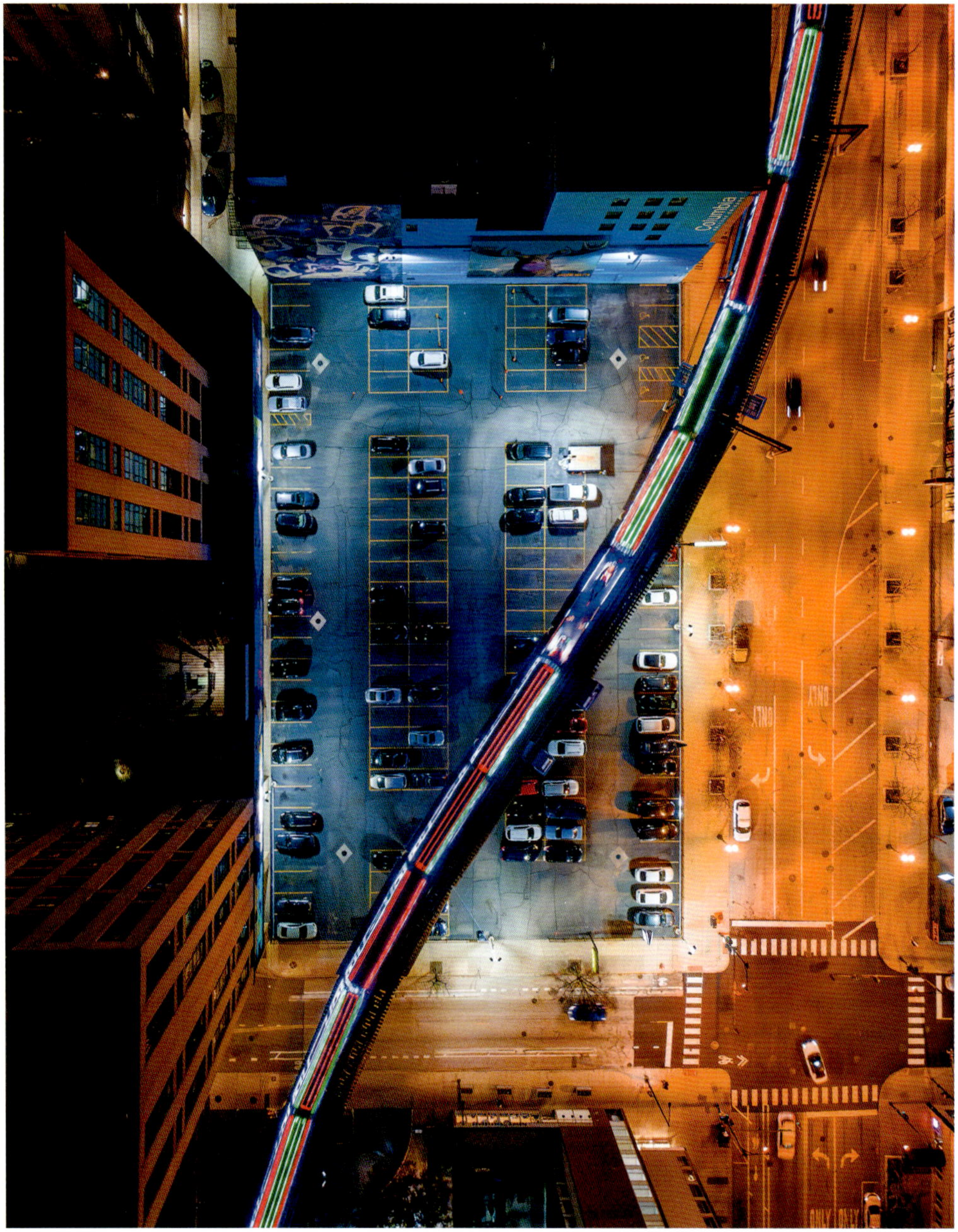

ABOVE: Over East Harrison Street and South Wabash Avenue **RIGHT:** Above West Institute Place and North Franklin Street

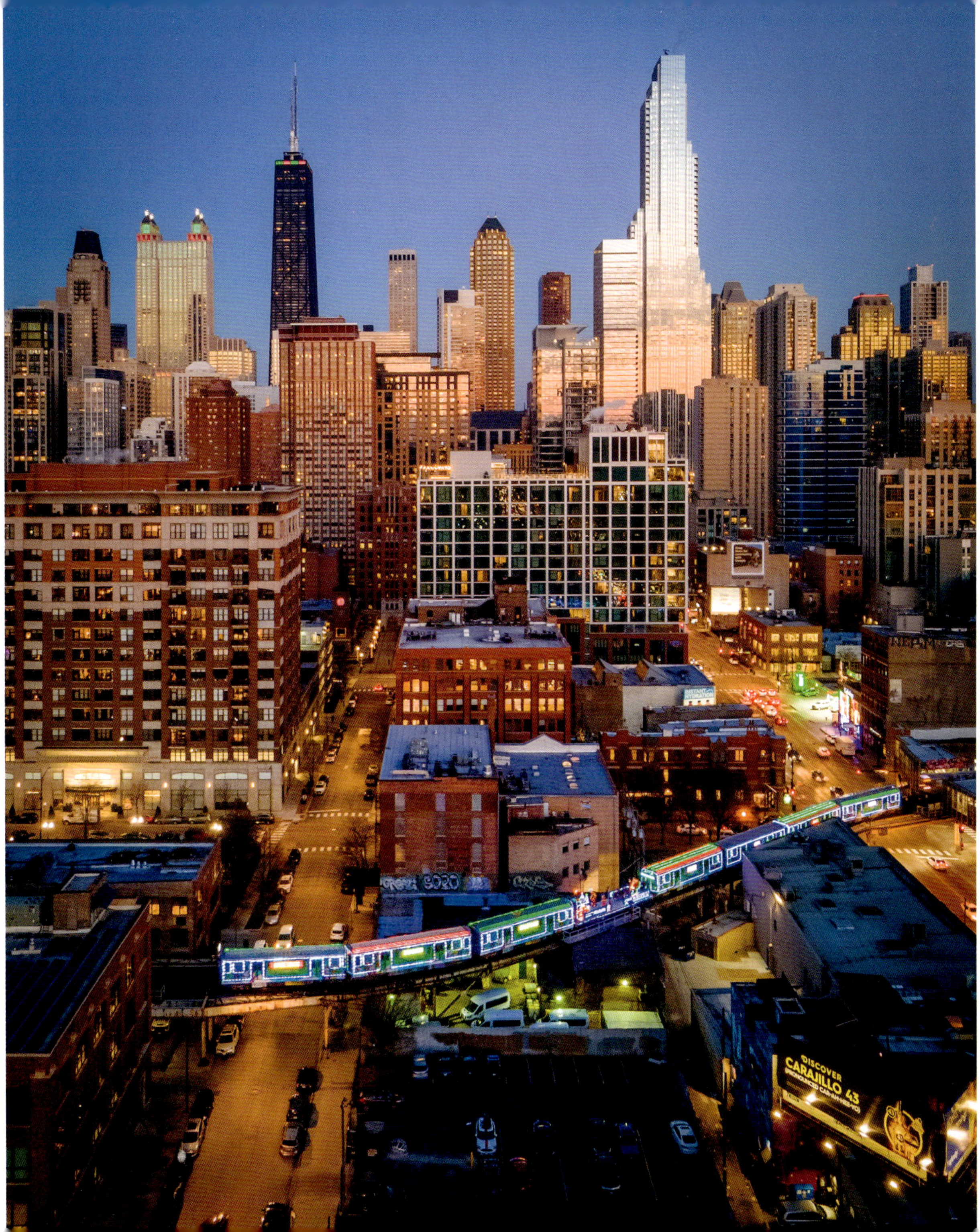
DISCOVER
CARAJILLO 43

The Holiday Train began on the Blue Line L train in 1992, but Santa and reindeer were added to the Holiday Train for the first time in 1995.

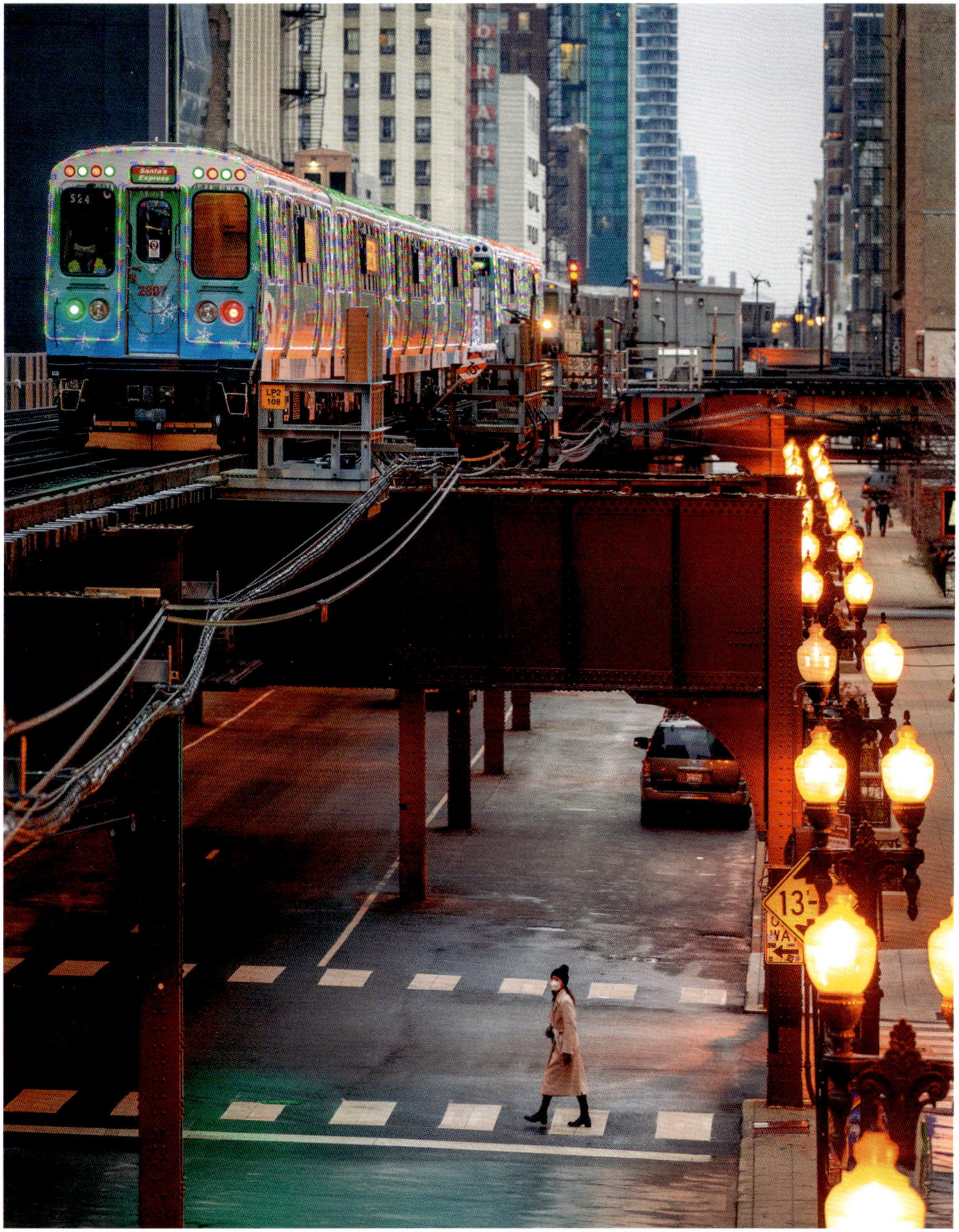

Looking down South Wabash Avenue

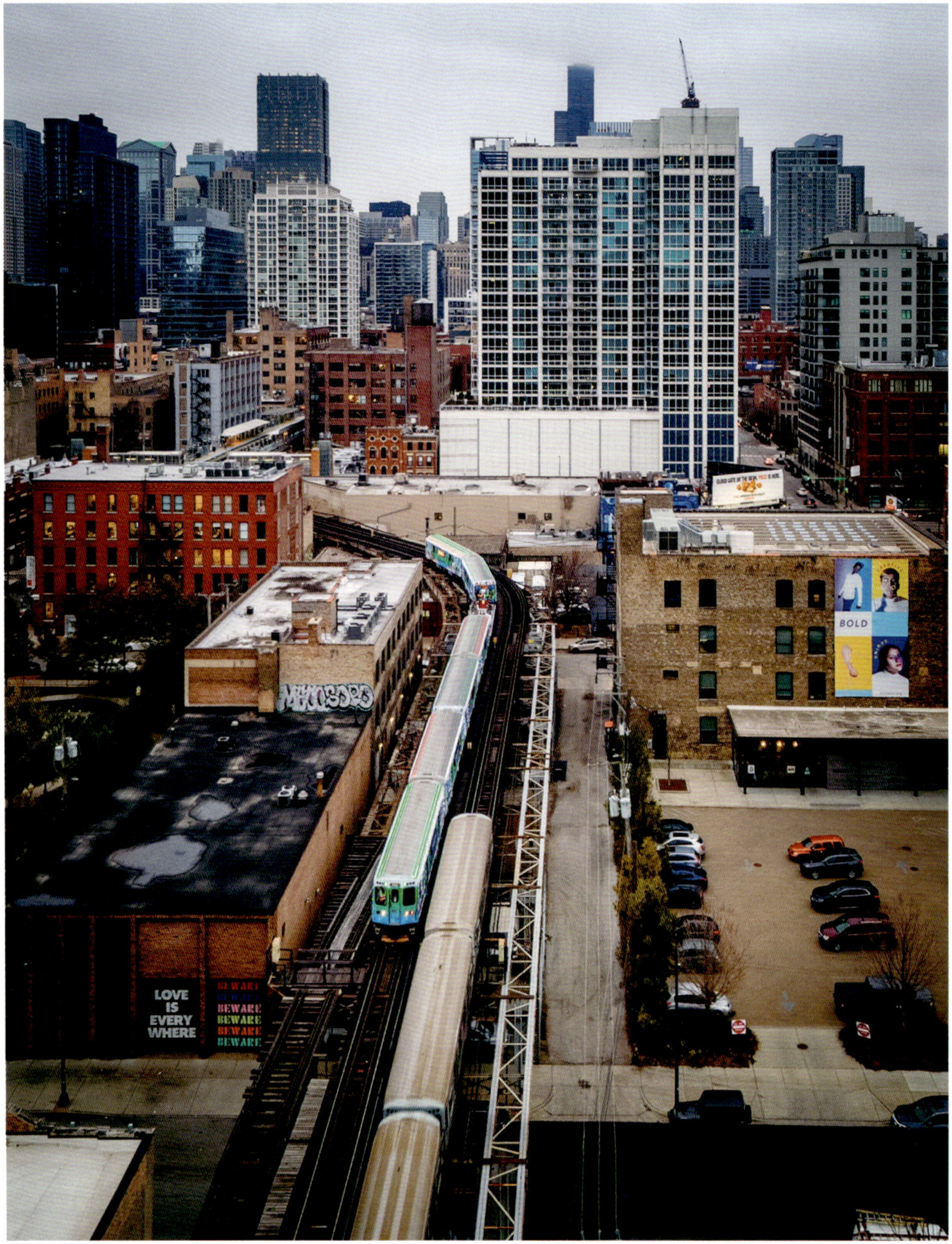

ABOVE: Over West Chestnut Street **RIGHT:** Looking down West Lake Street

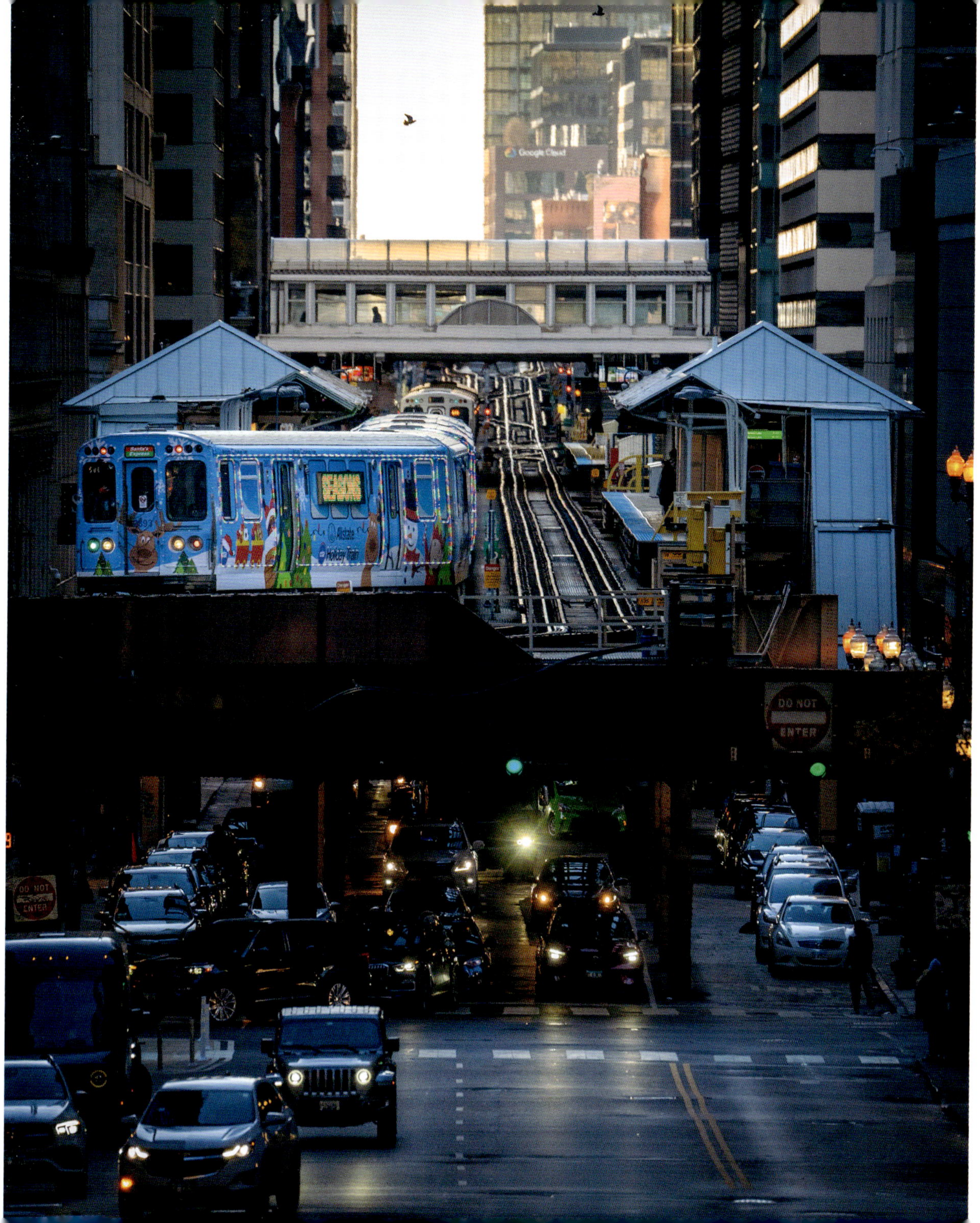
Google Cloud
DO NOT ENTER
DO NOT ENTER

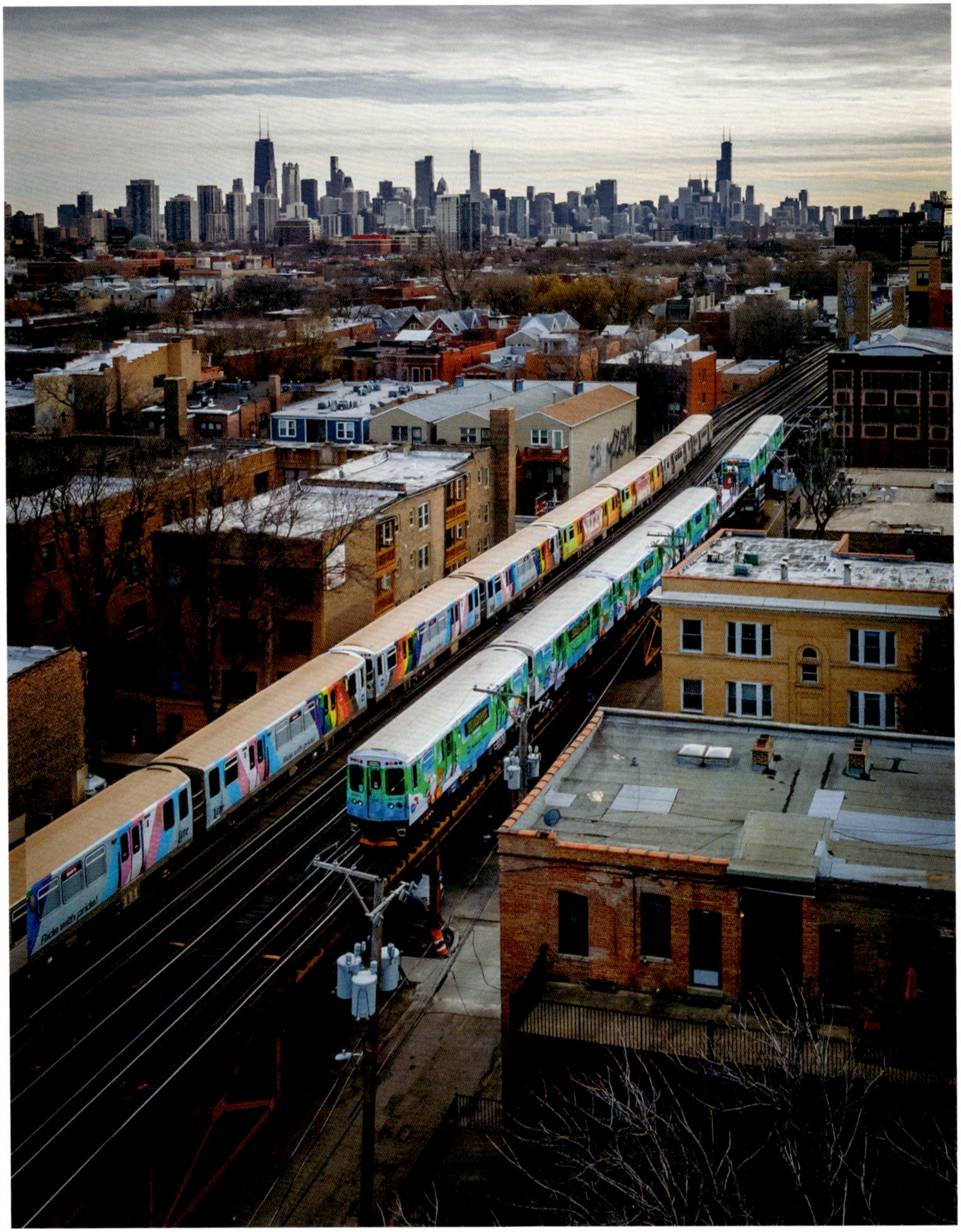

ABOVE: Skyline view from Ravenswood **RIGHT:** Above North Clark Street and North Sheffield Avenue

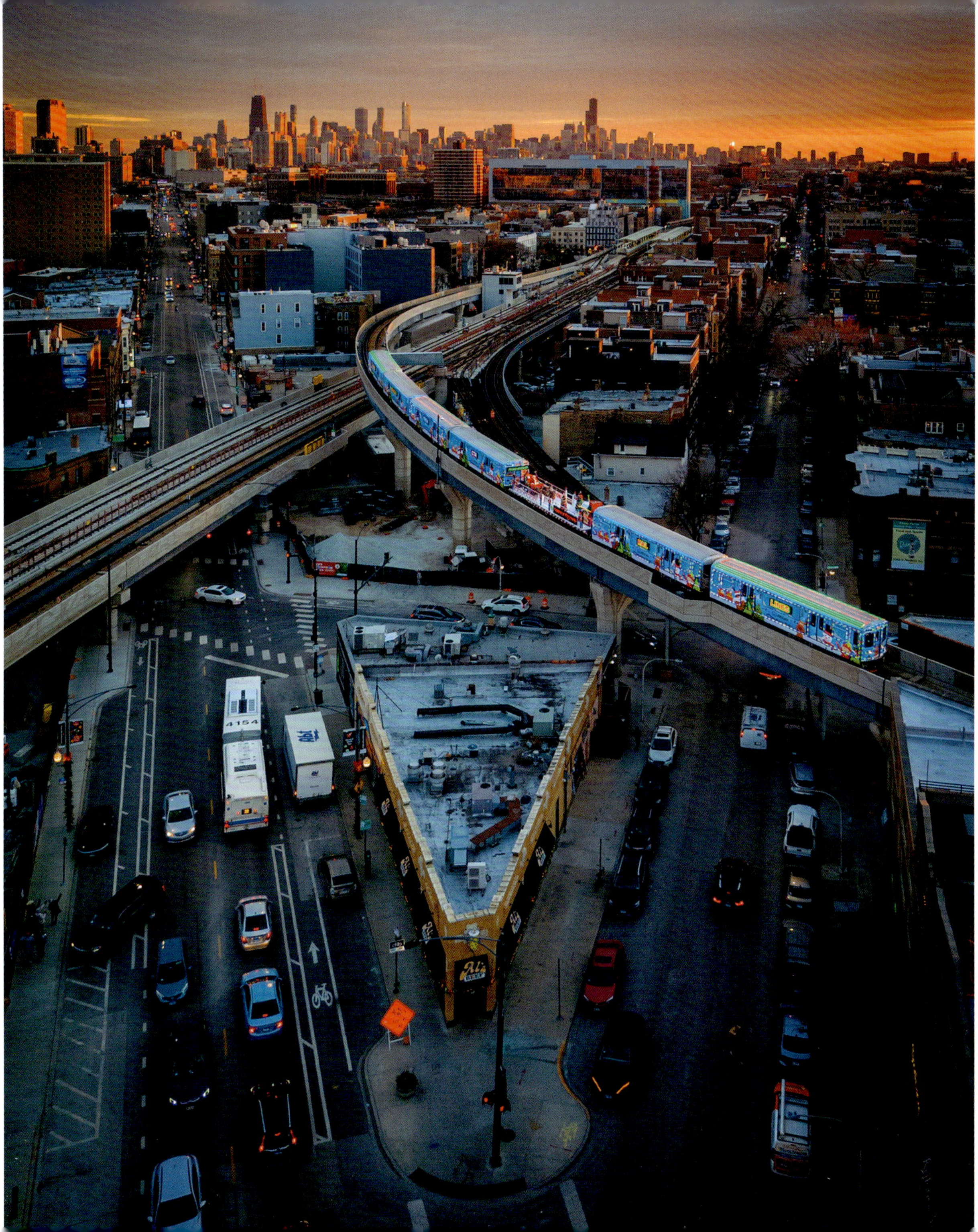
4154

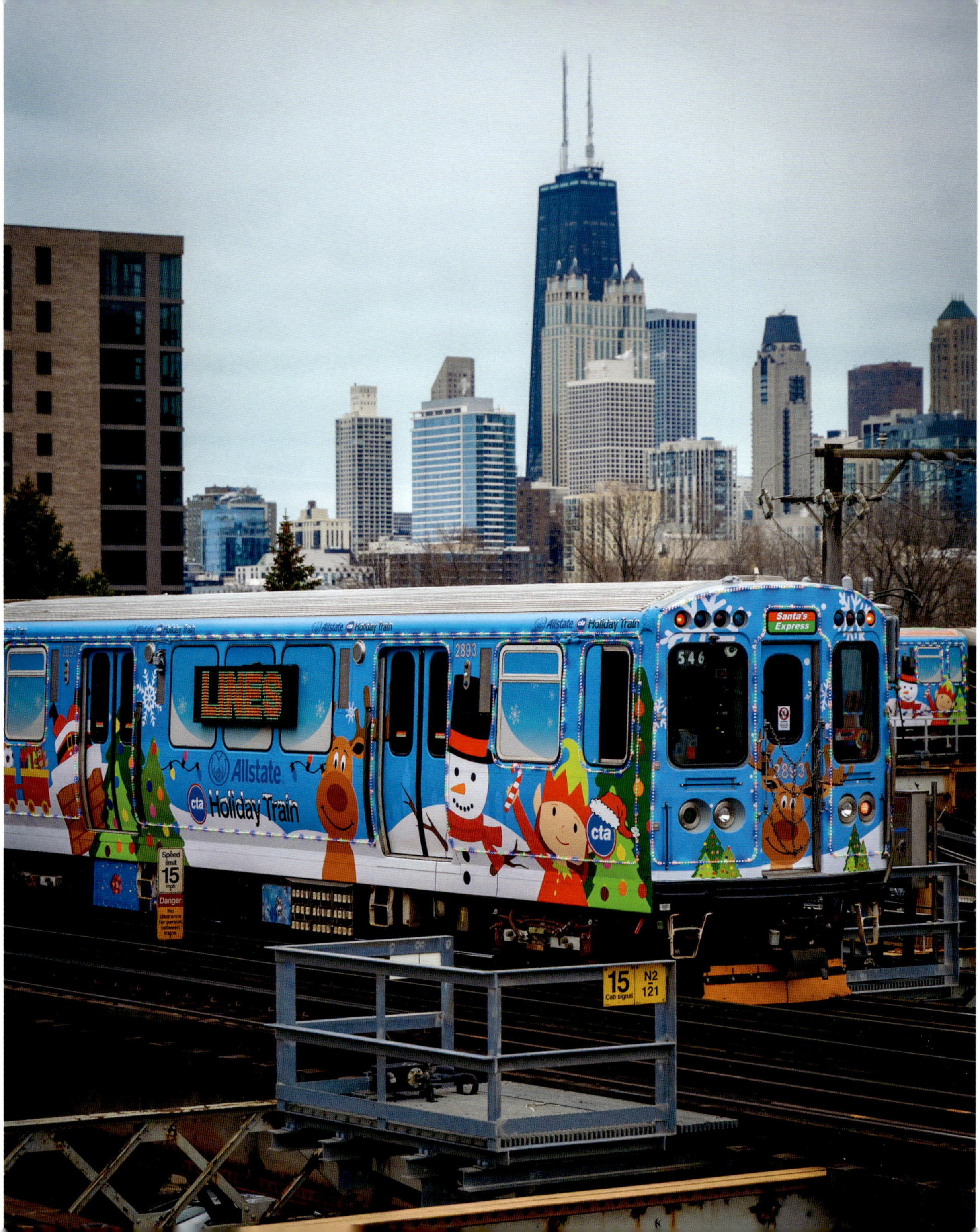
LINES
Allstate
cta Holiday Train
Santa's Express
546
2893
Speed limit 15 mph
Danger
15 Cab signal
N2 121

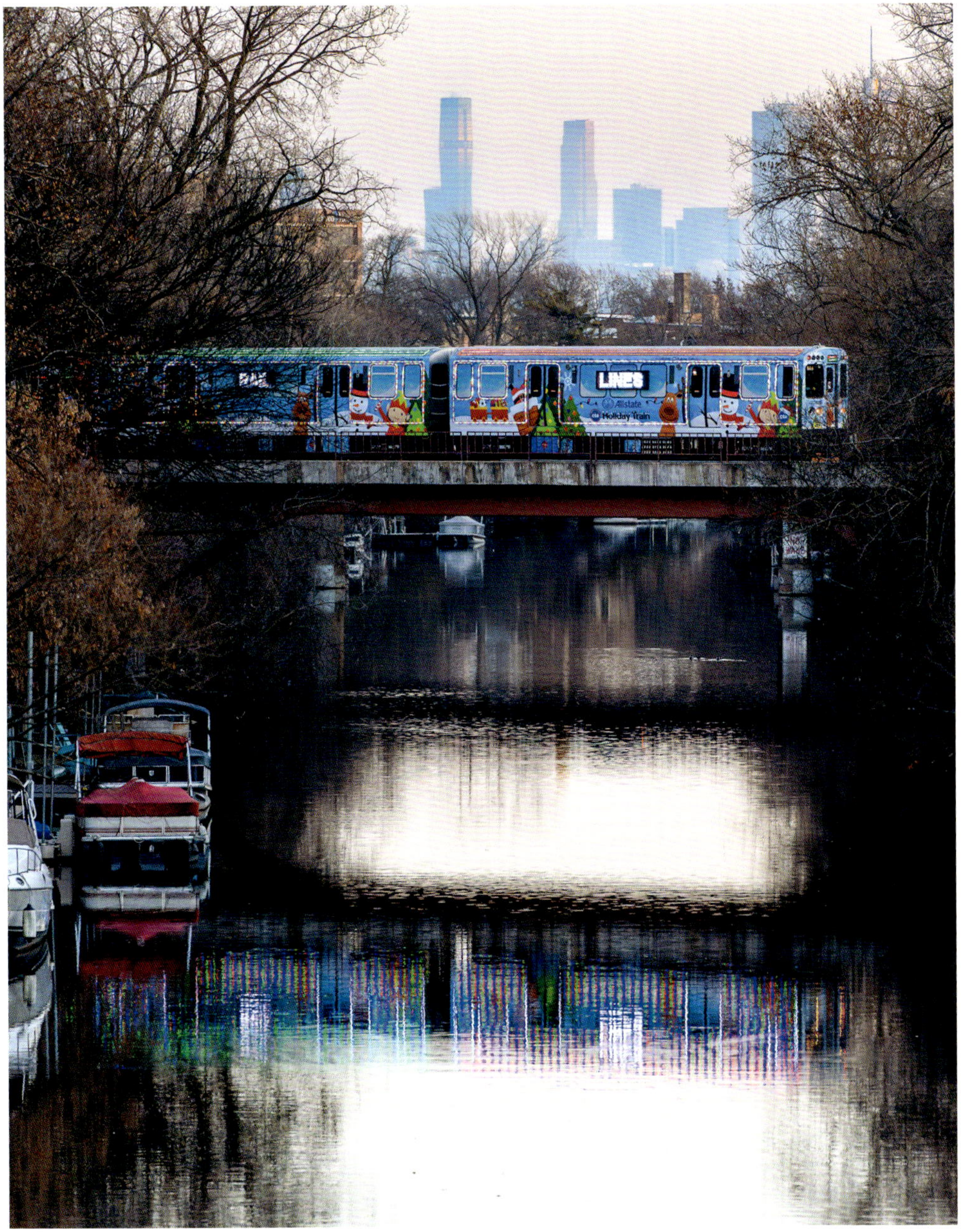

LEFT: Skyline view from North Halsted Street **ABOVE:** CTA Holiday Train over the North Branch Chicago River

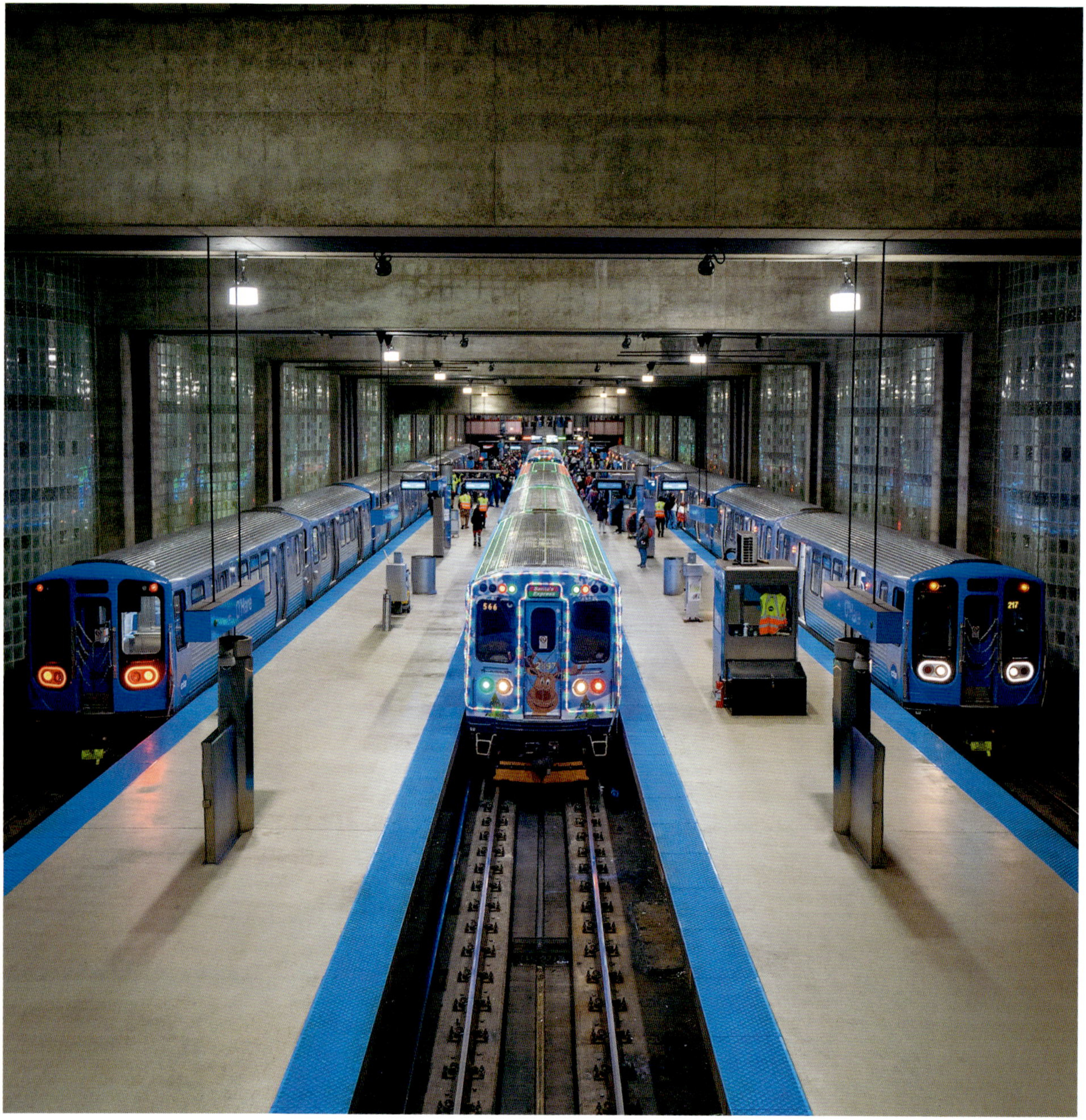

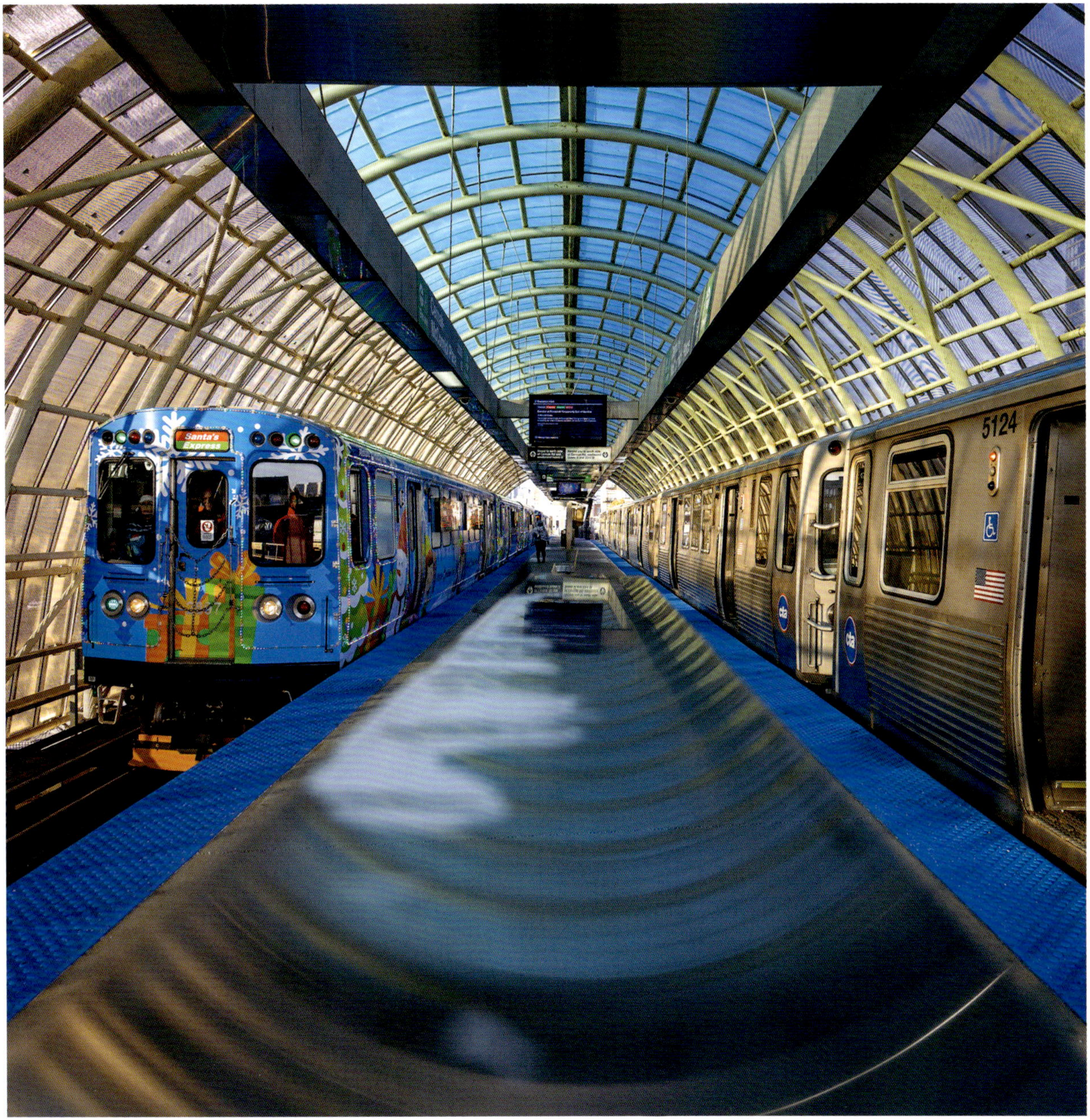

Inside Cermak-McCormick Place station

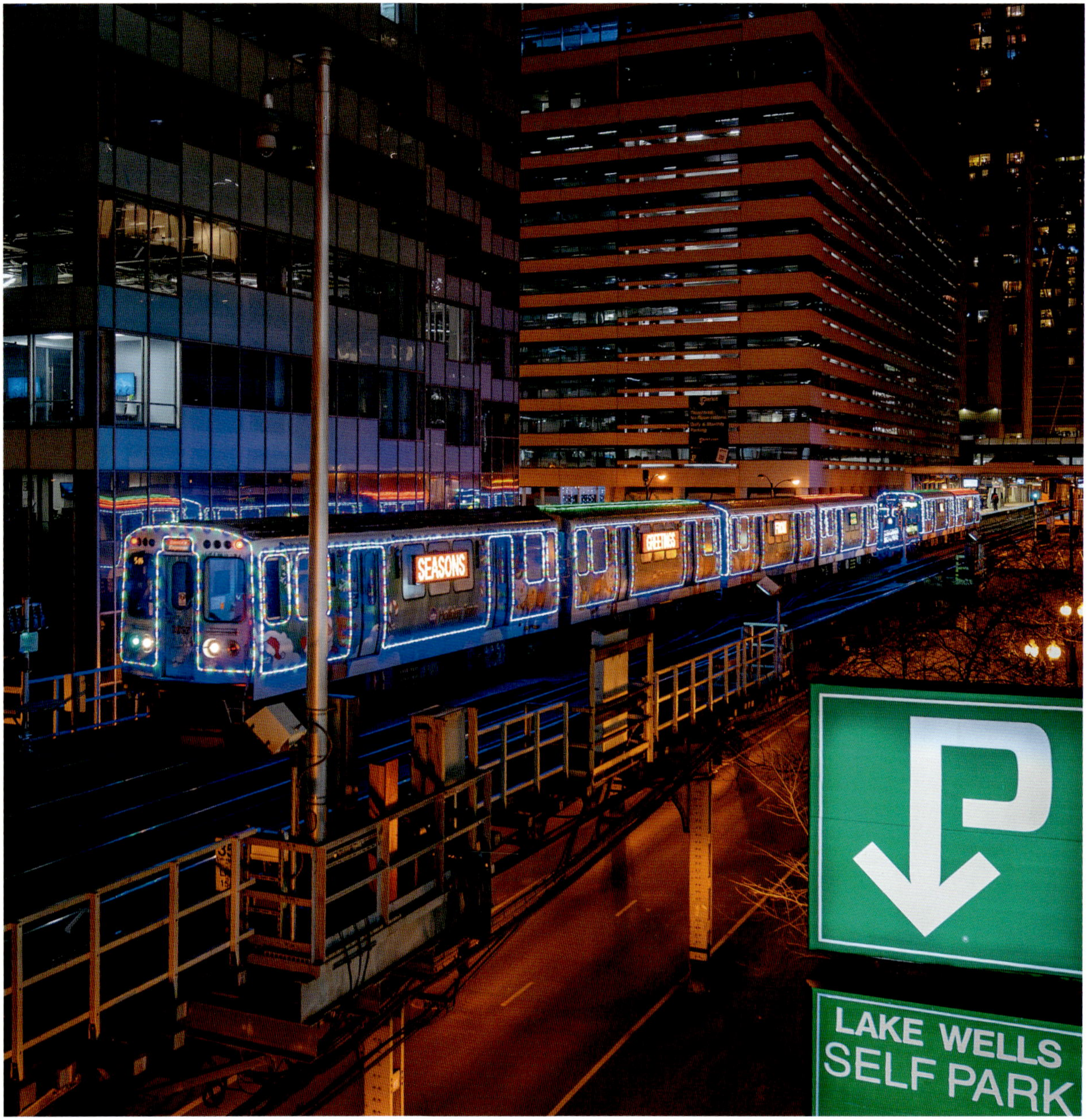

Looking down North Wells Street

The holidays shine bright in Chicago. Thousands of colorful lights outline the shape of the Holiday Train and adorn its windows, with even more lights running across the tops of each train's six cars.

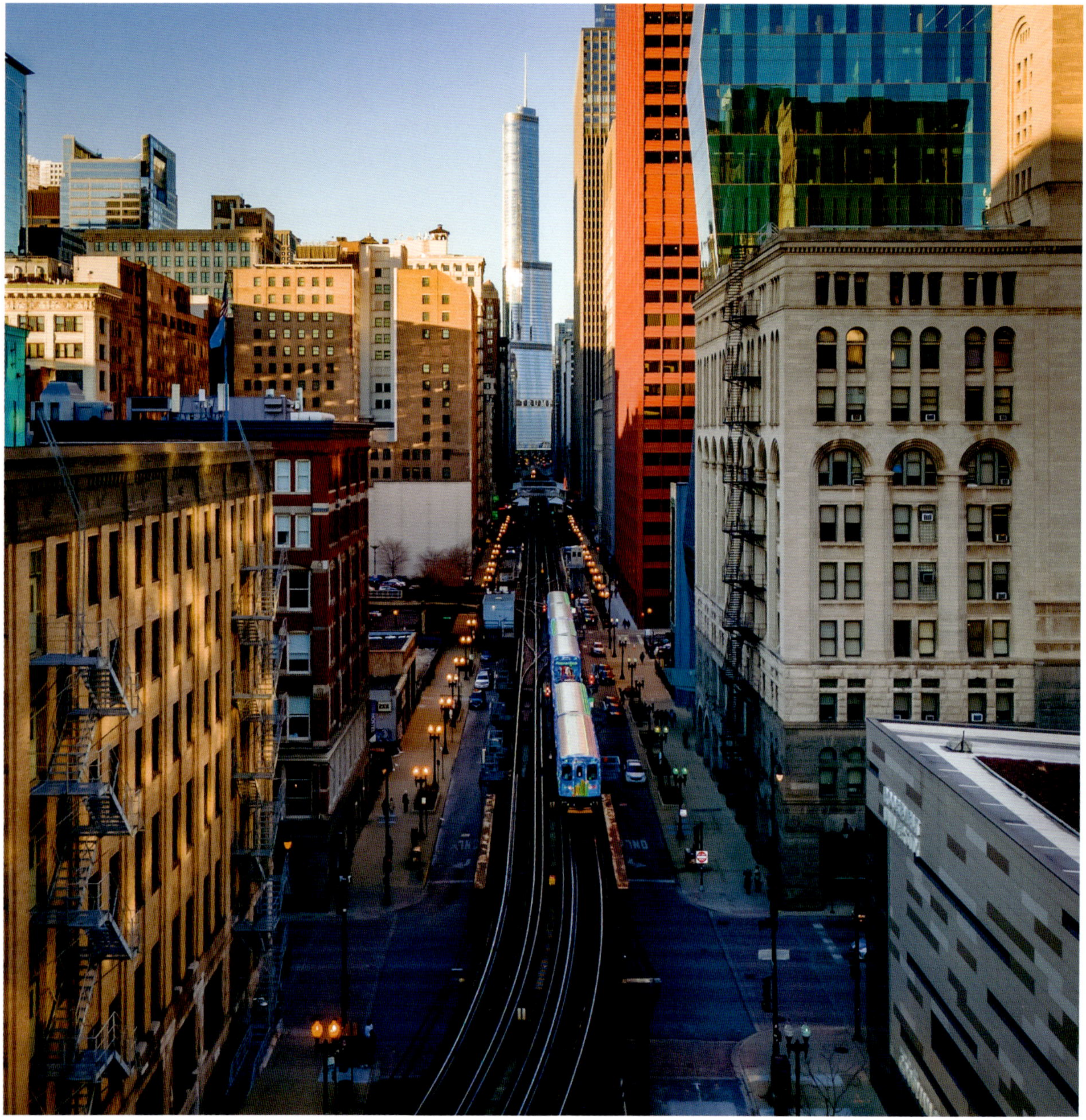

ABOVE: Over South Wabash Avenue **RIGHT:** Above East Harrison Street and South Wabash Avenue

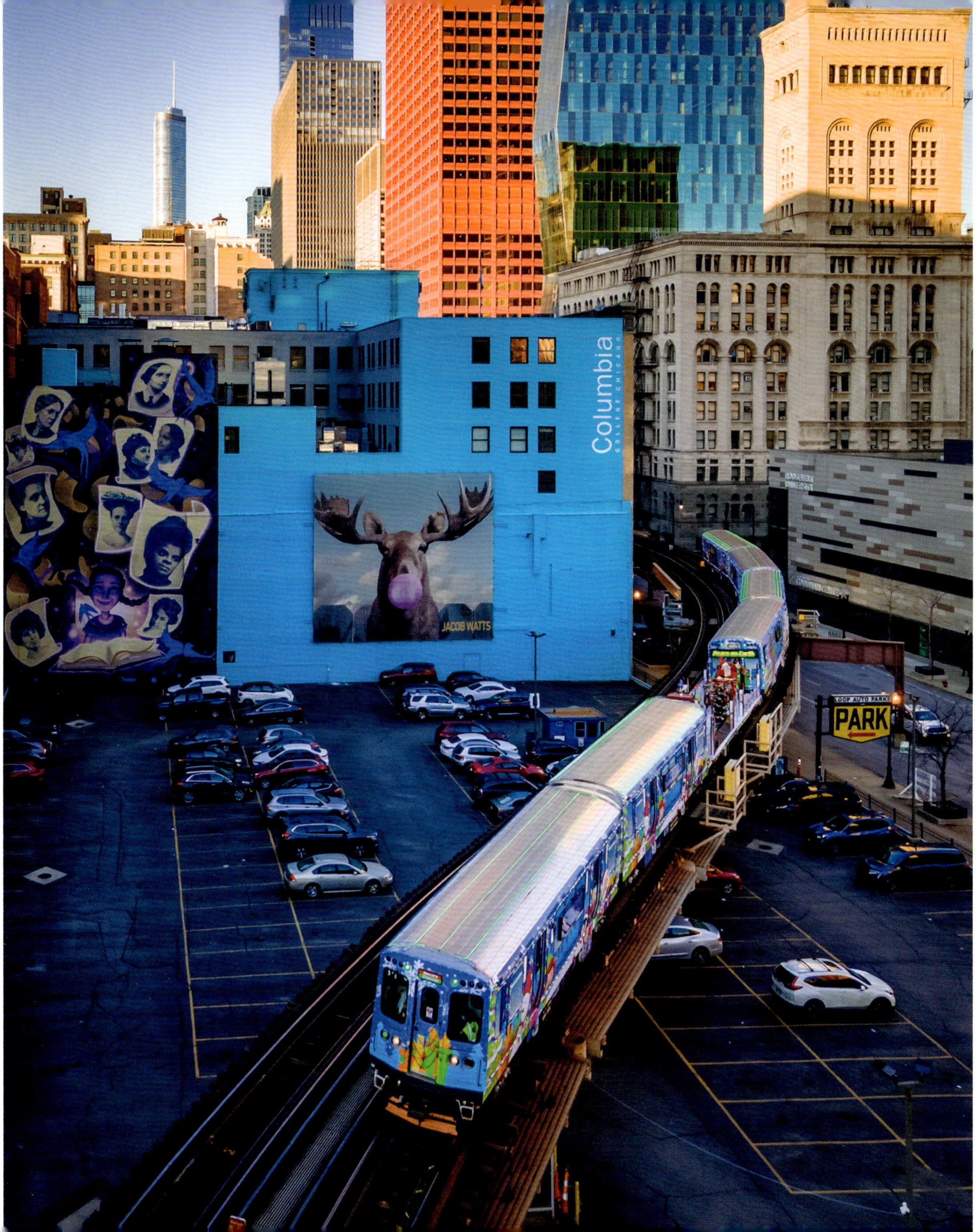
Columbia
JACOB WATTS
PARK

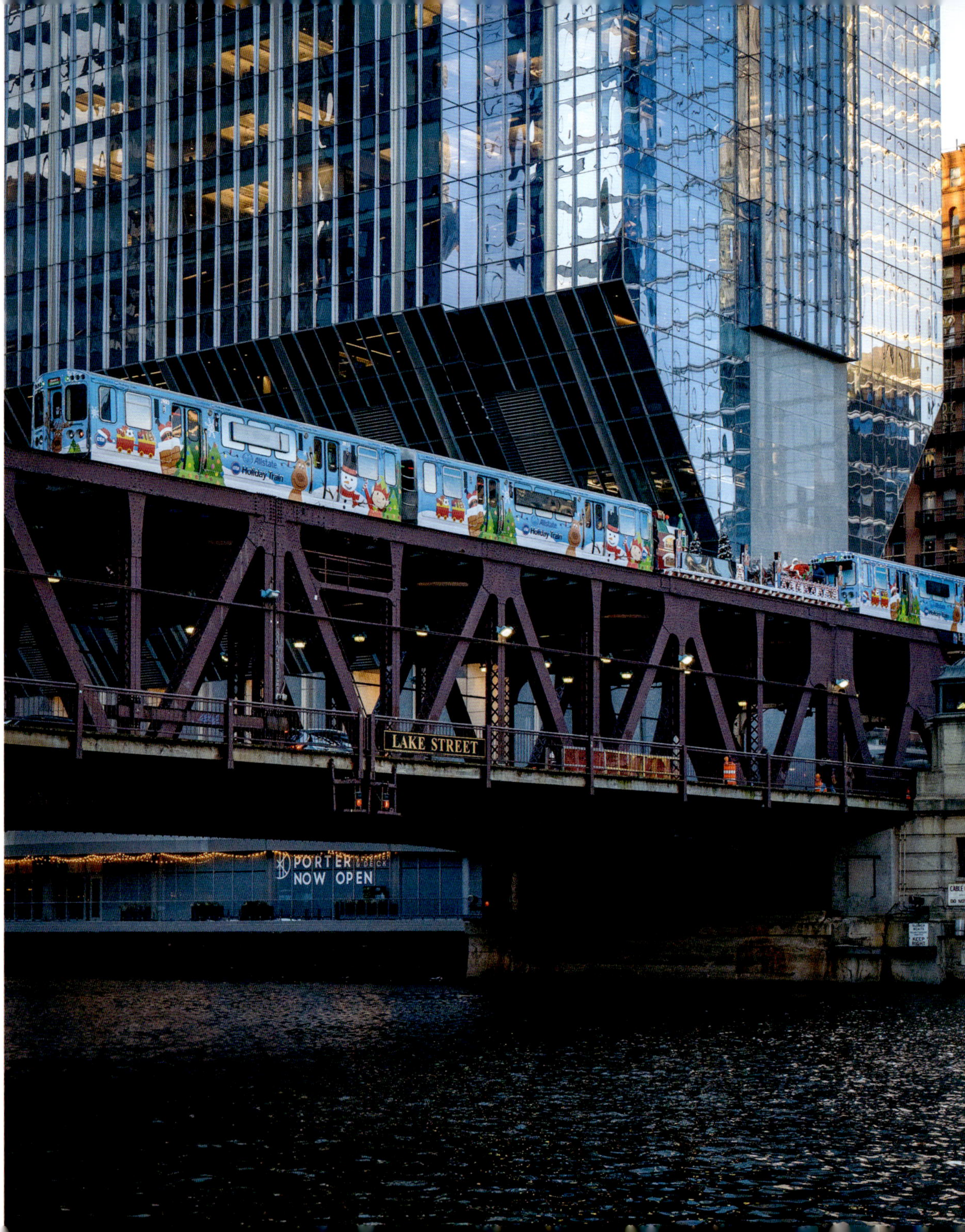
LAKE STREET
PORTER
NOW OPEN
Allstate
Holiday Train

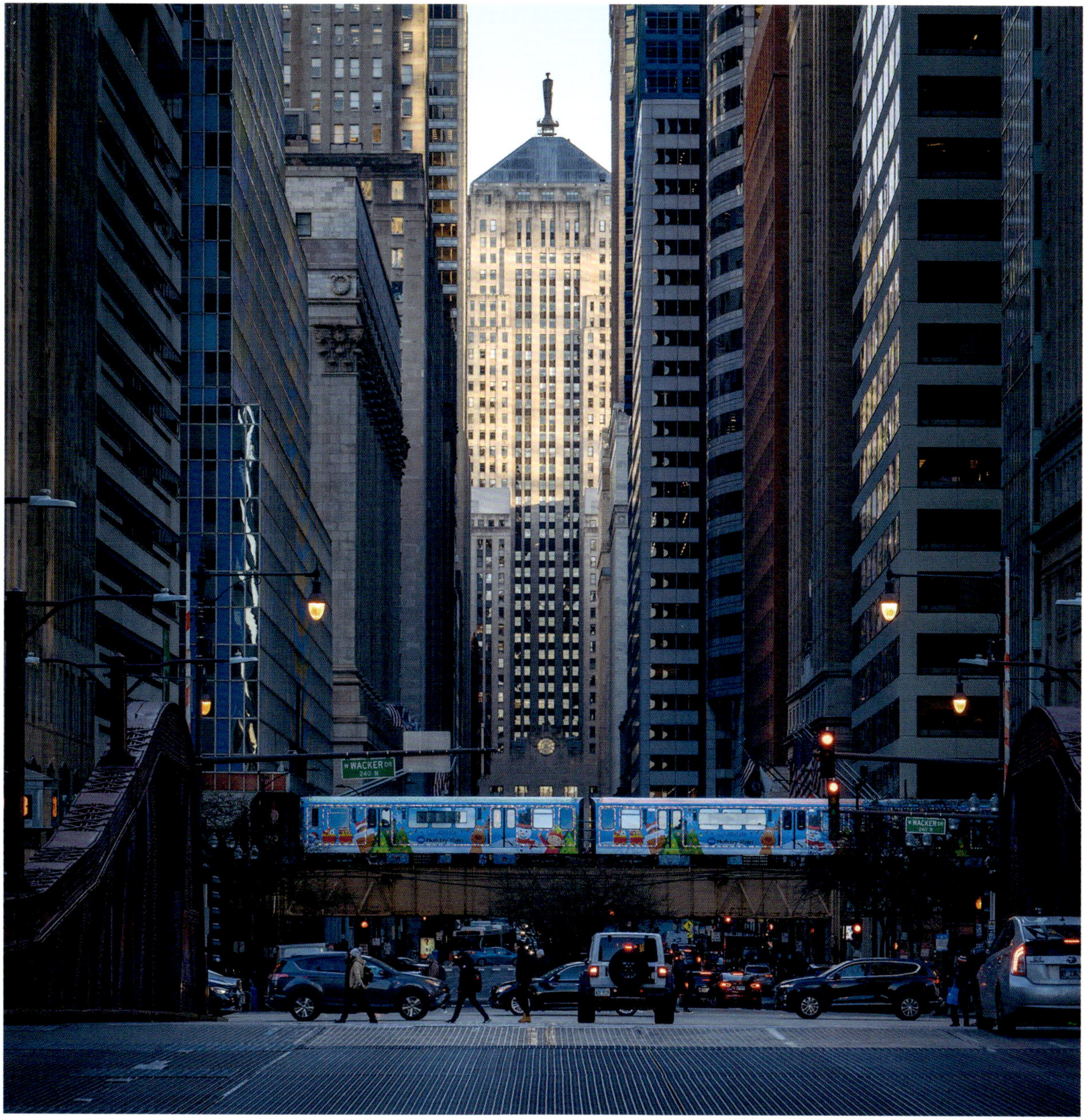

LEFT: View of Lake Street Bridge **ABOVE:** Looking down North LaSalle Street

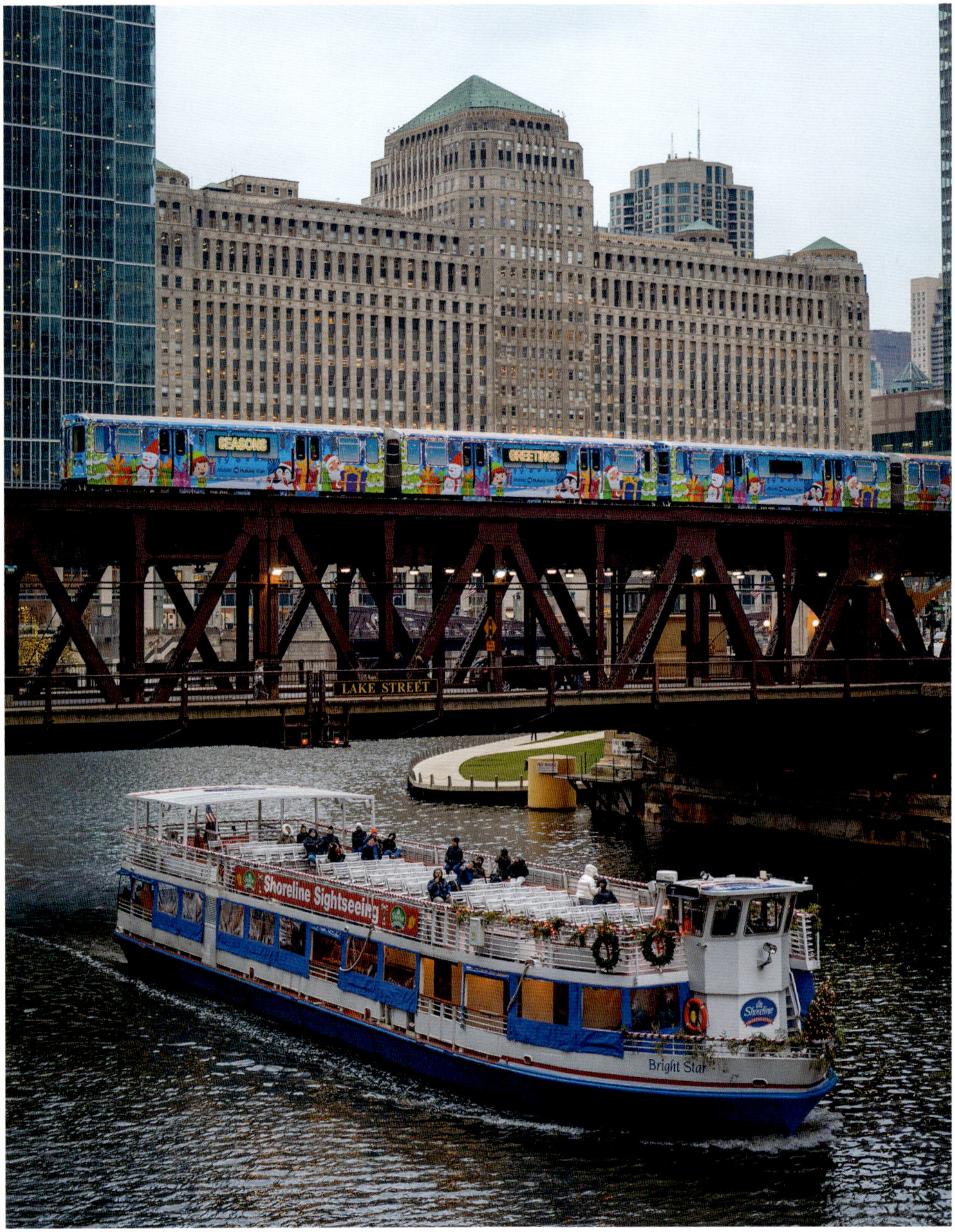

ABOVE: View of Lake Street Bridge and the Merchandise Mart **RIGHT:** Above Lake Street

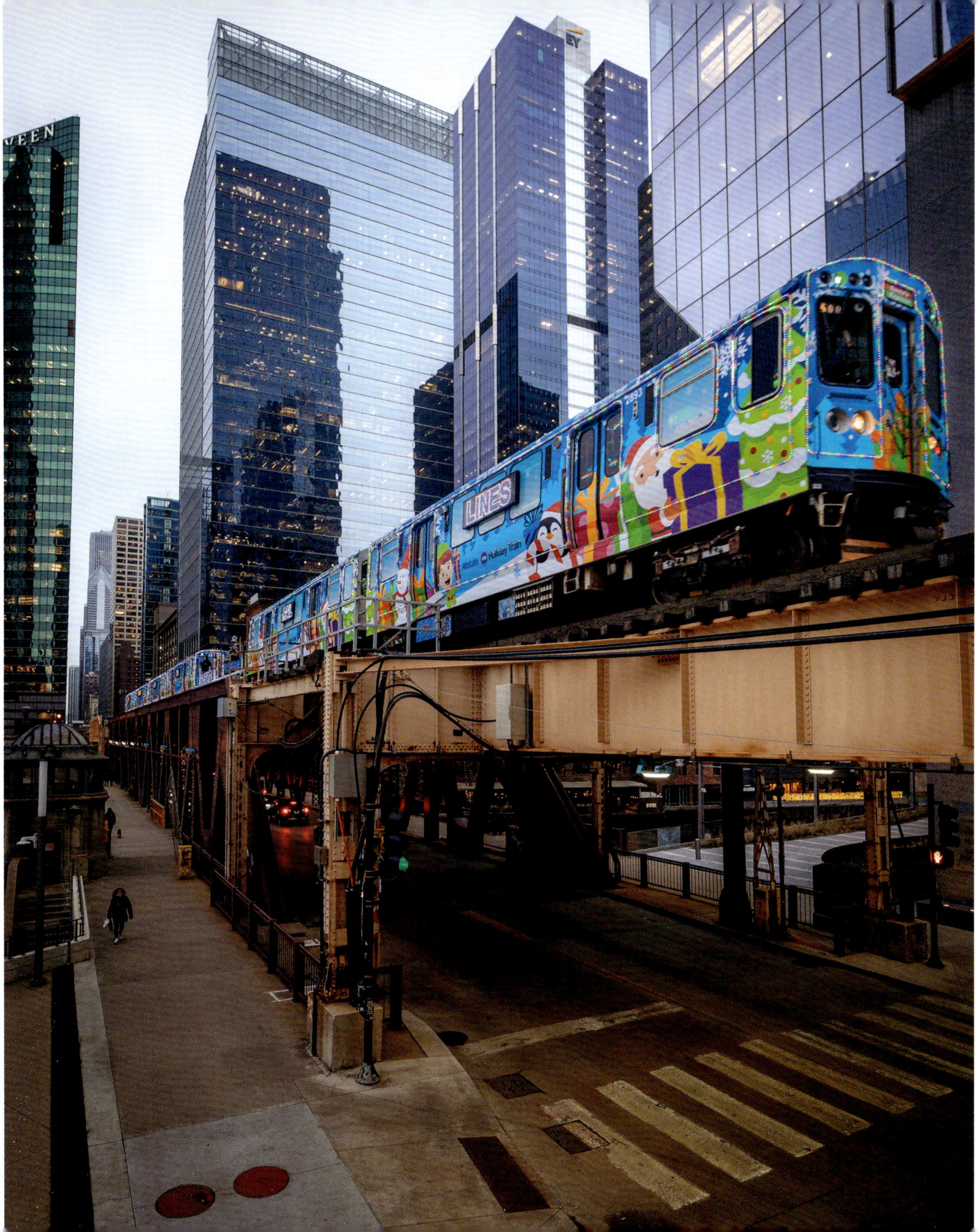
VEEN
EY
LINES

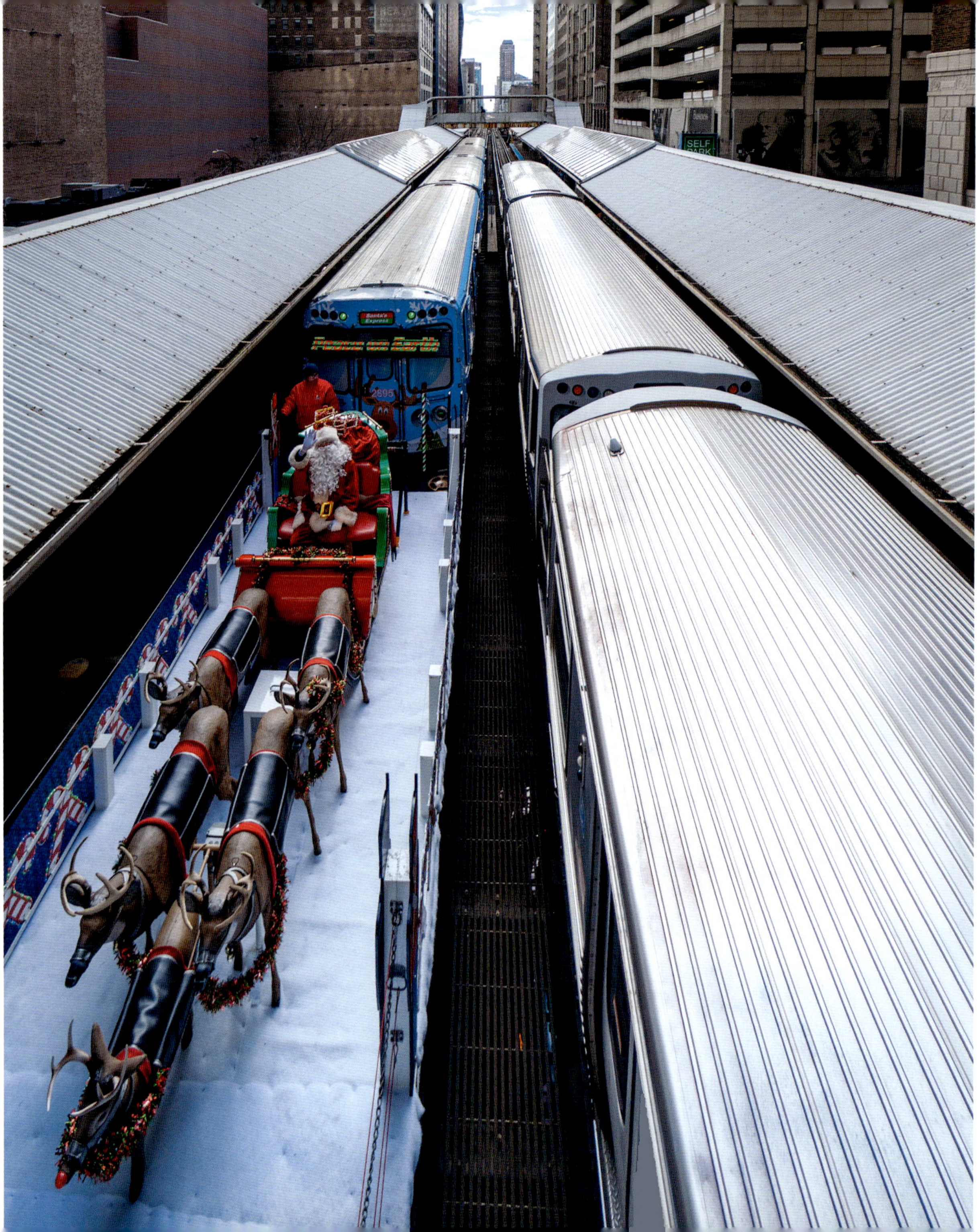
Santa's
Express
2895

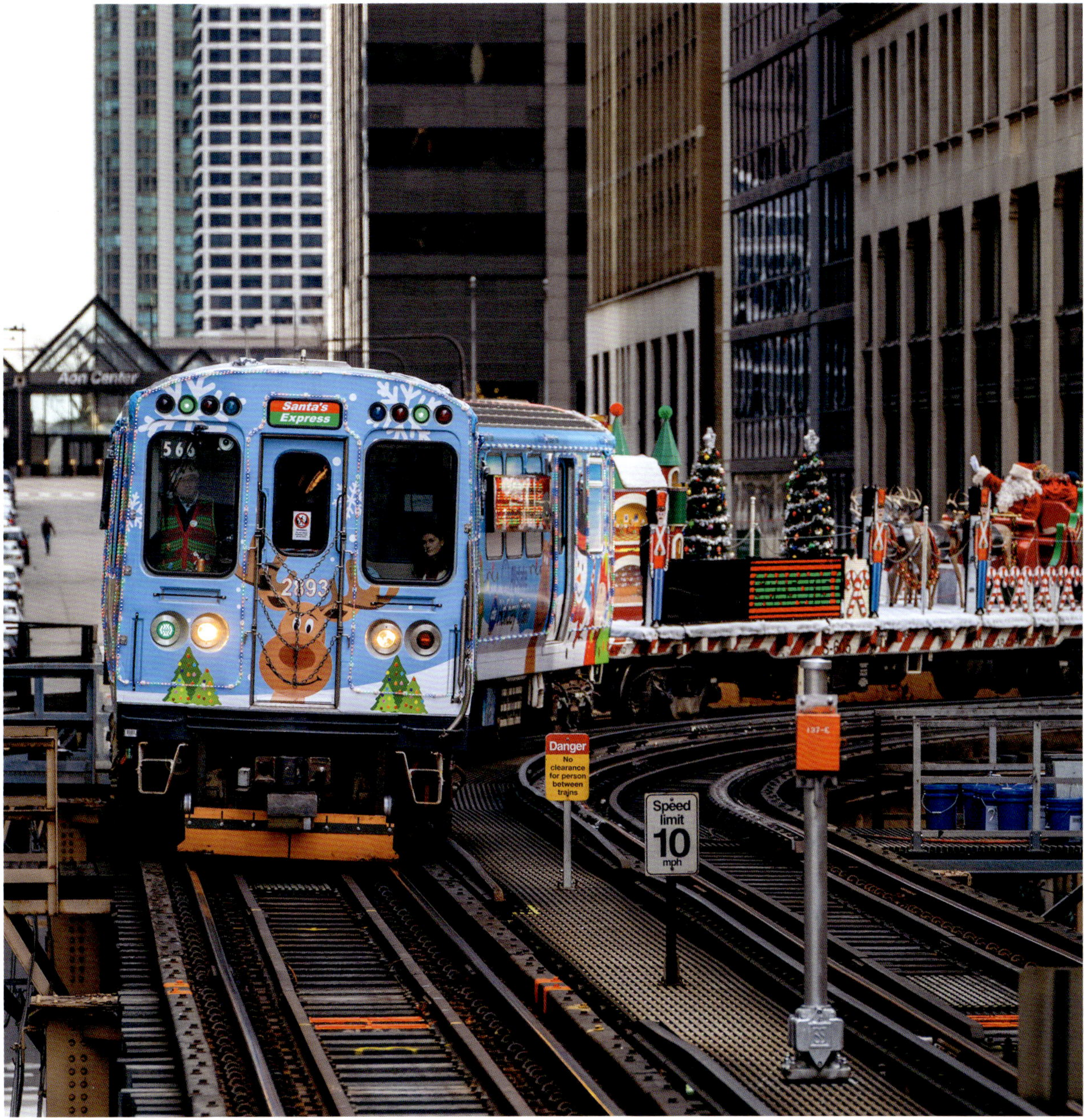

LEFT: Above Adams/Wabash station **ABOVE:** Approaching Stake/Lake station

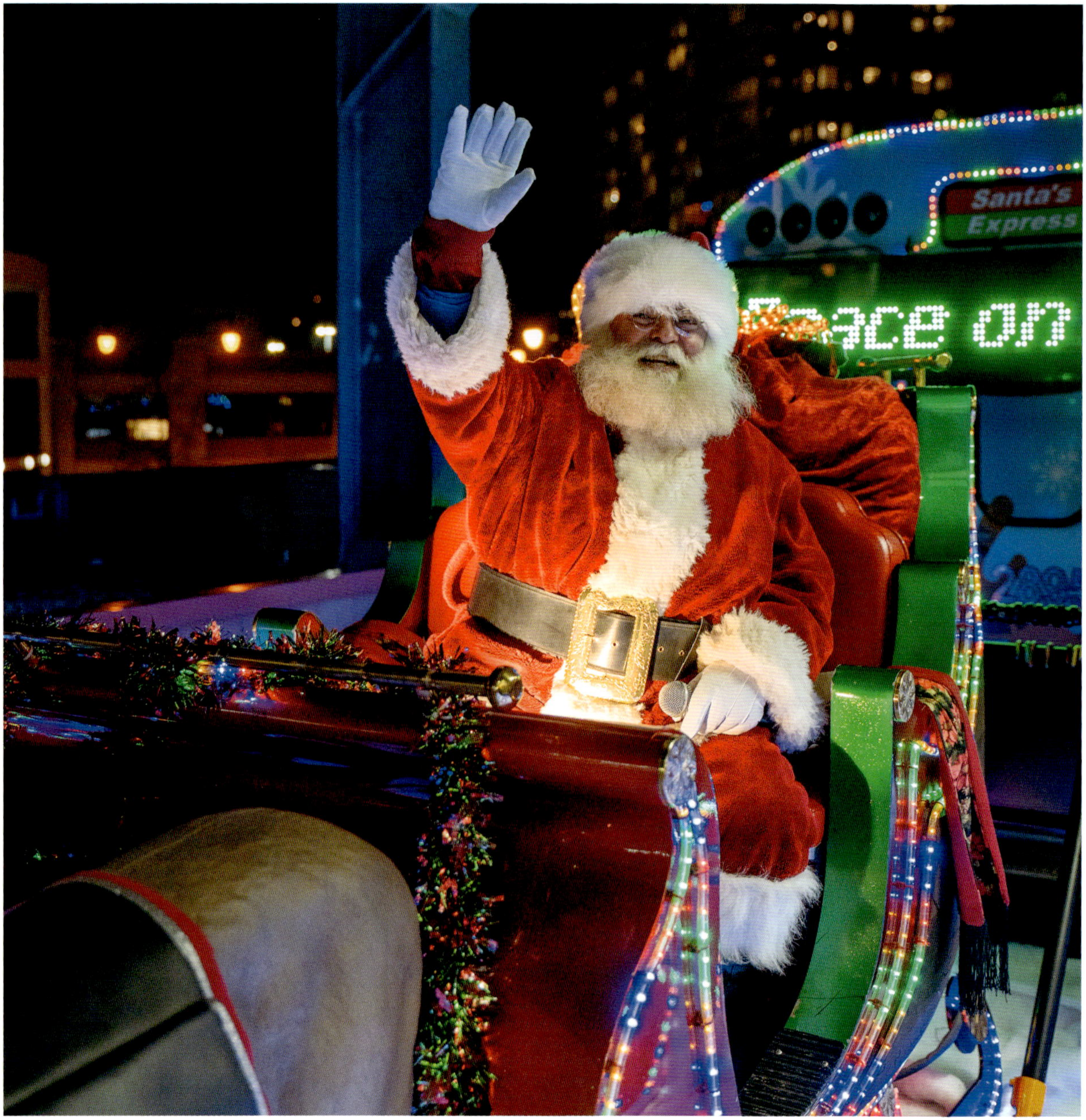

Santa on the CTA Holiday Train

Through wind, snow, and rain, Santa stays outside for each train run—and doesn't go inside between station visits.

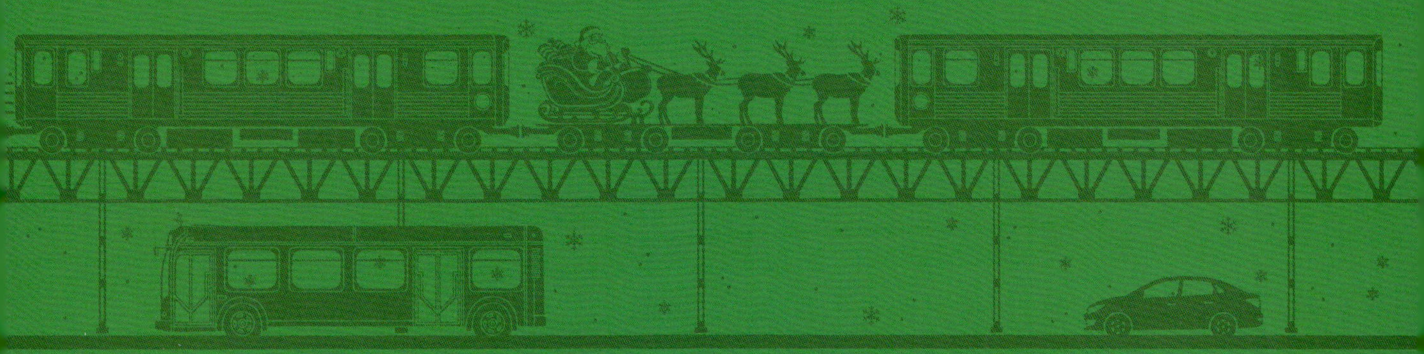

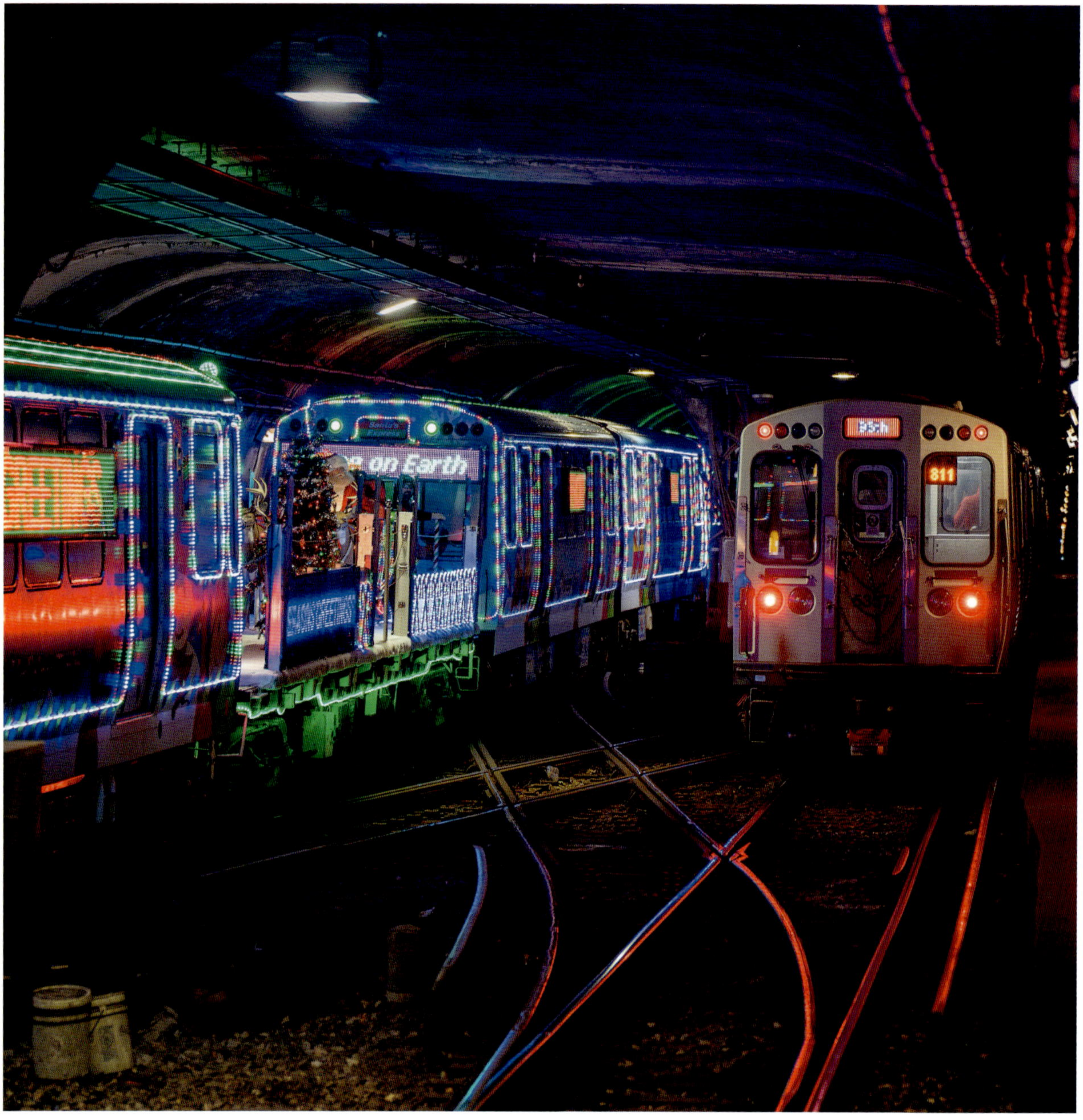

ABOVE & RIGHT: Inside the CTA Tunnels

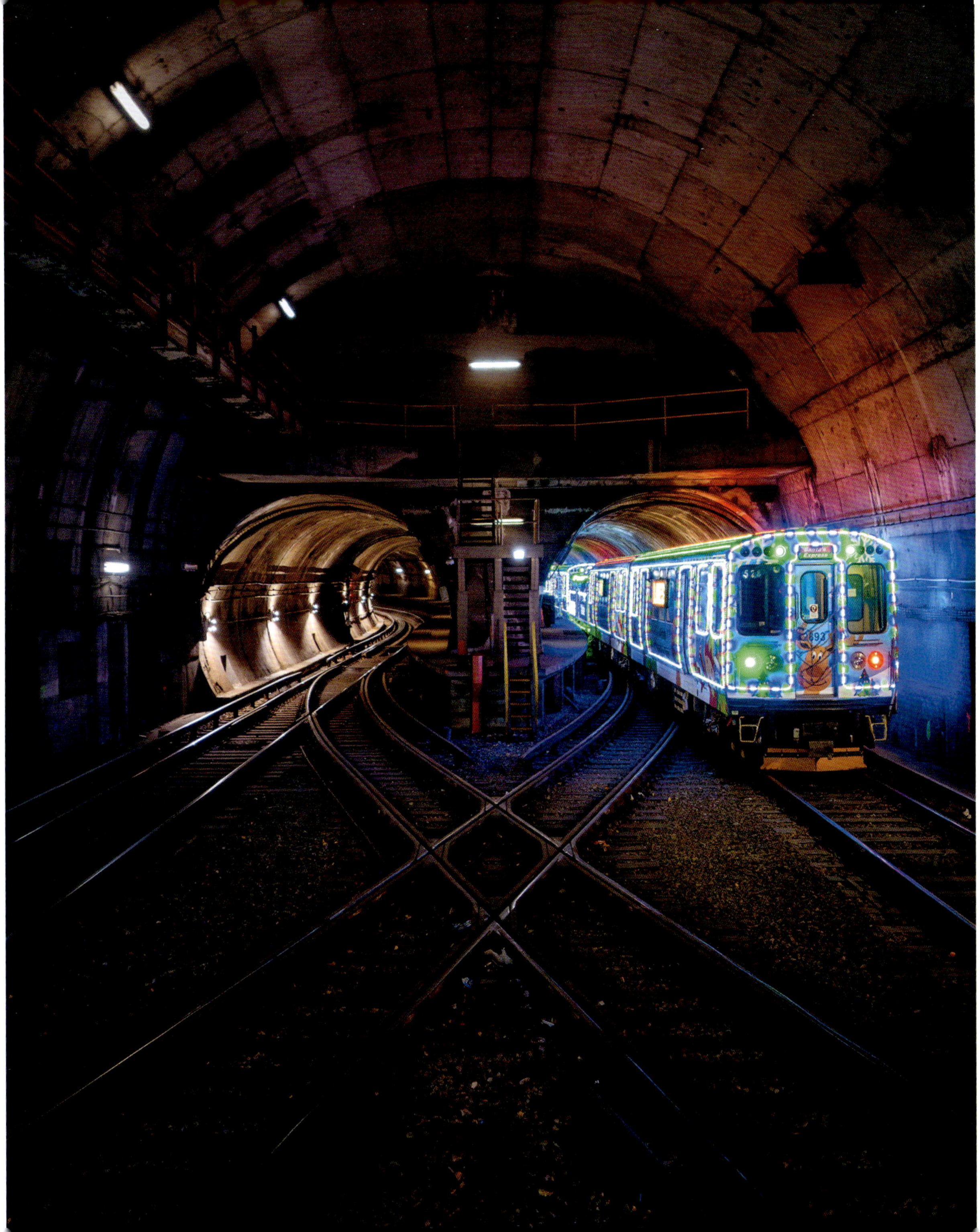

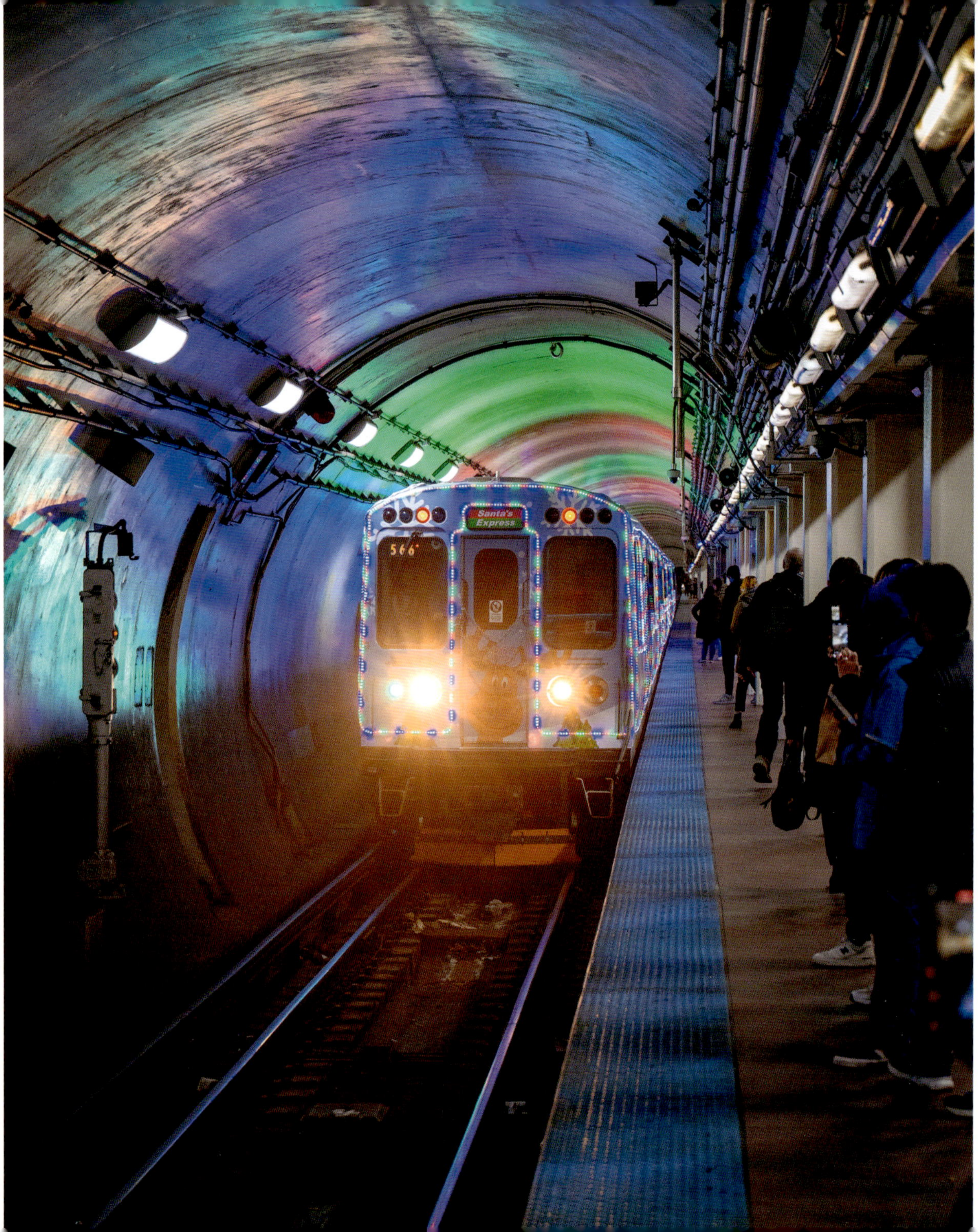
Santa's Express
566

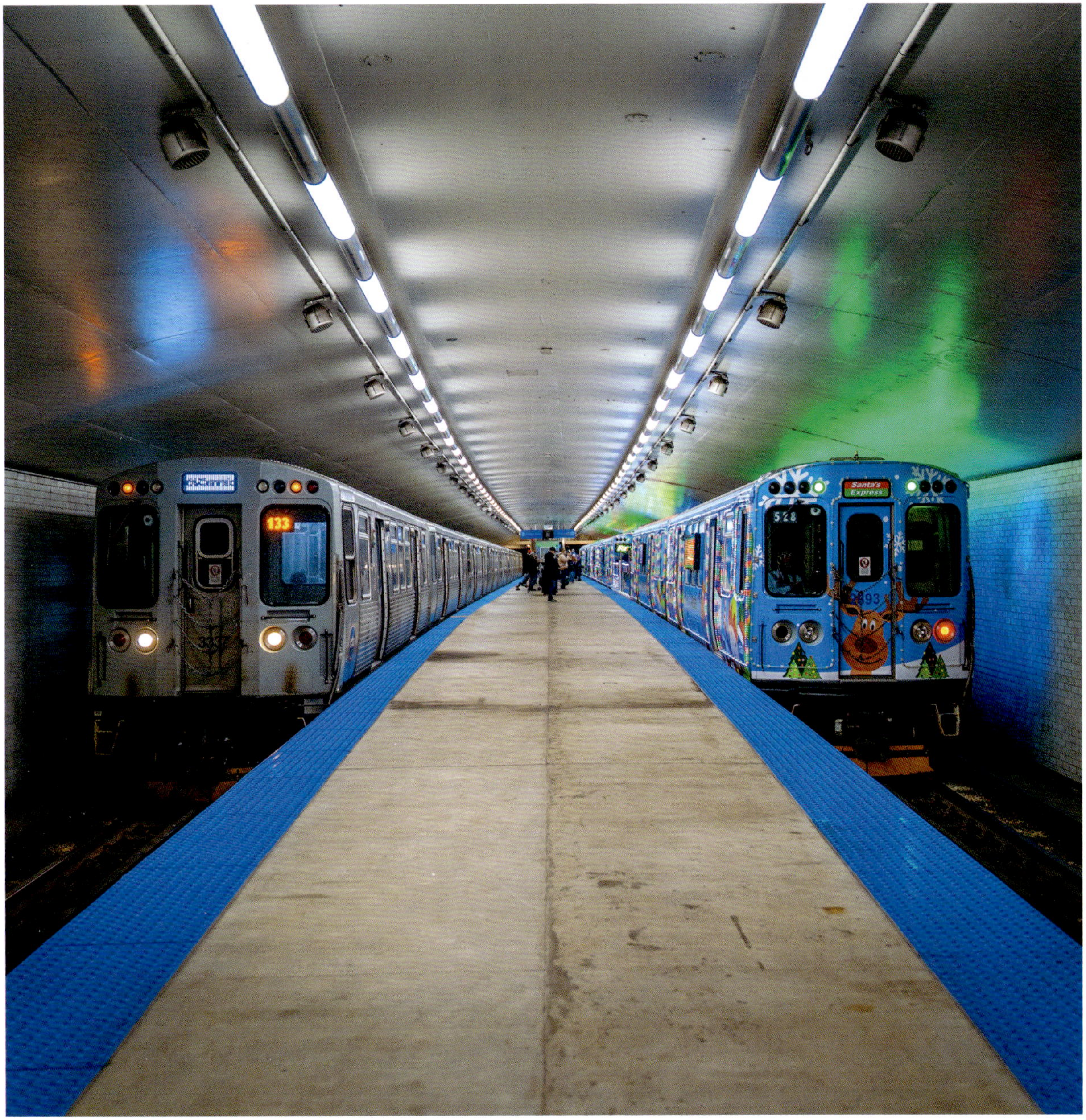

LEFT: Approaching an underground CTA station **ABOVE:** Inside Belmont station

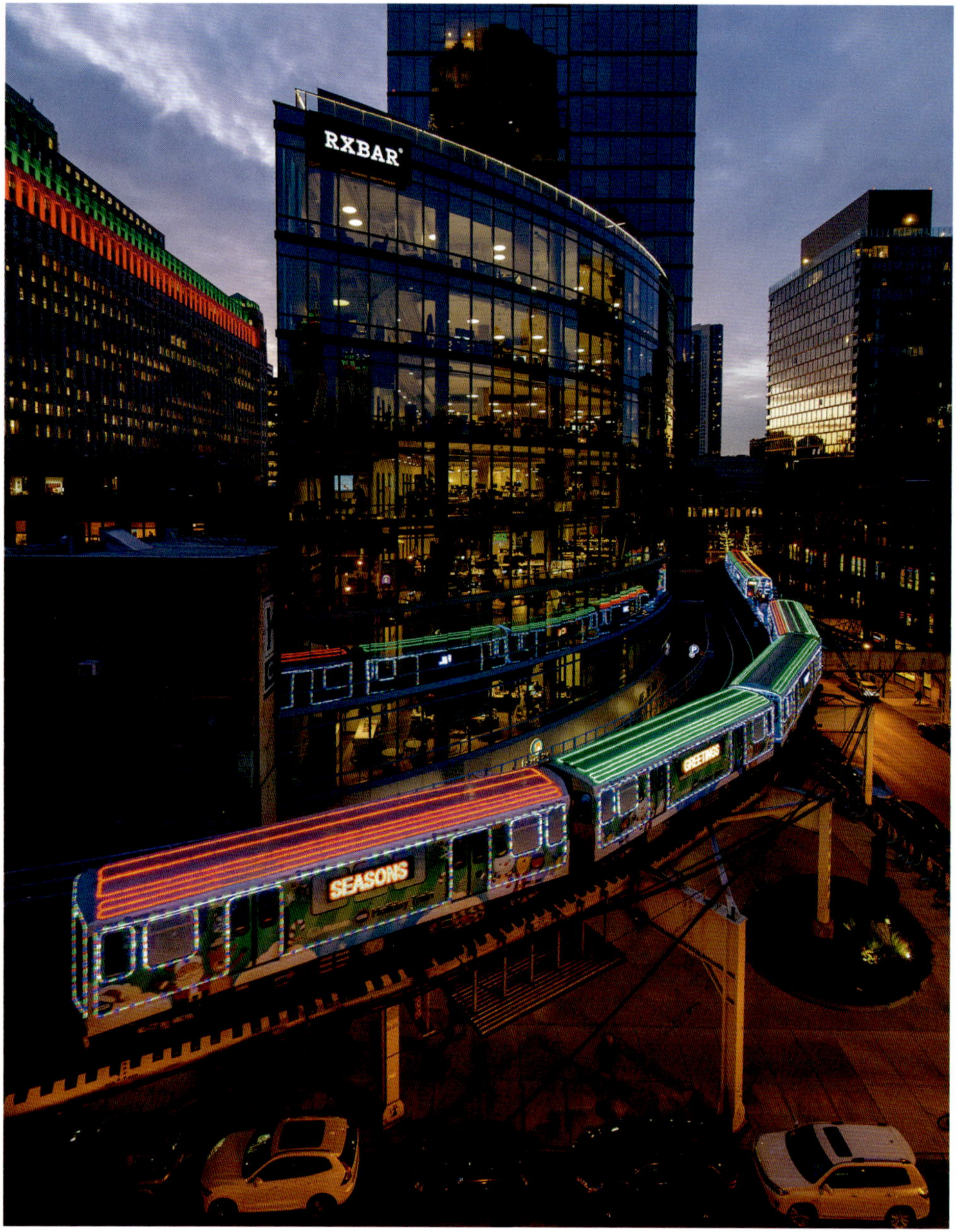

ABOVE: Over North Wells Street and West Hubbard Street **RIGHT:** View from Margaret Hie Ding Lin Park

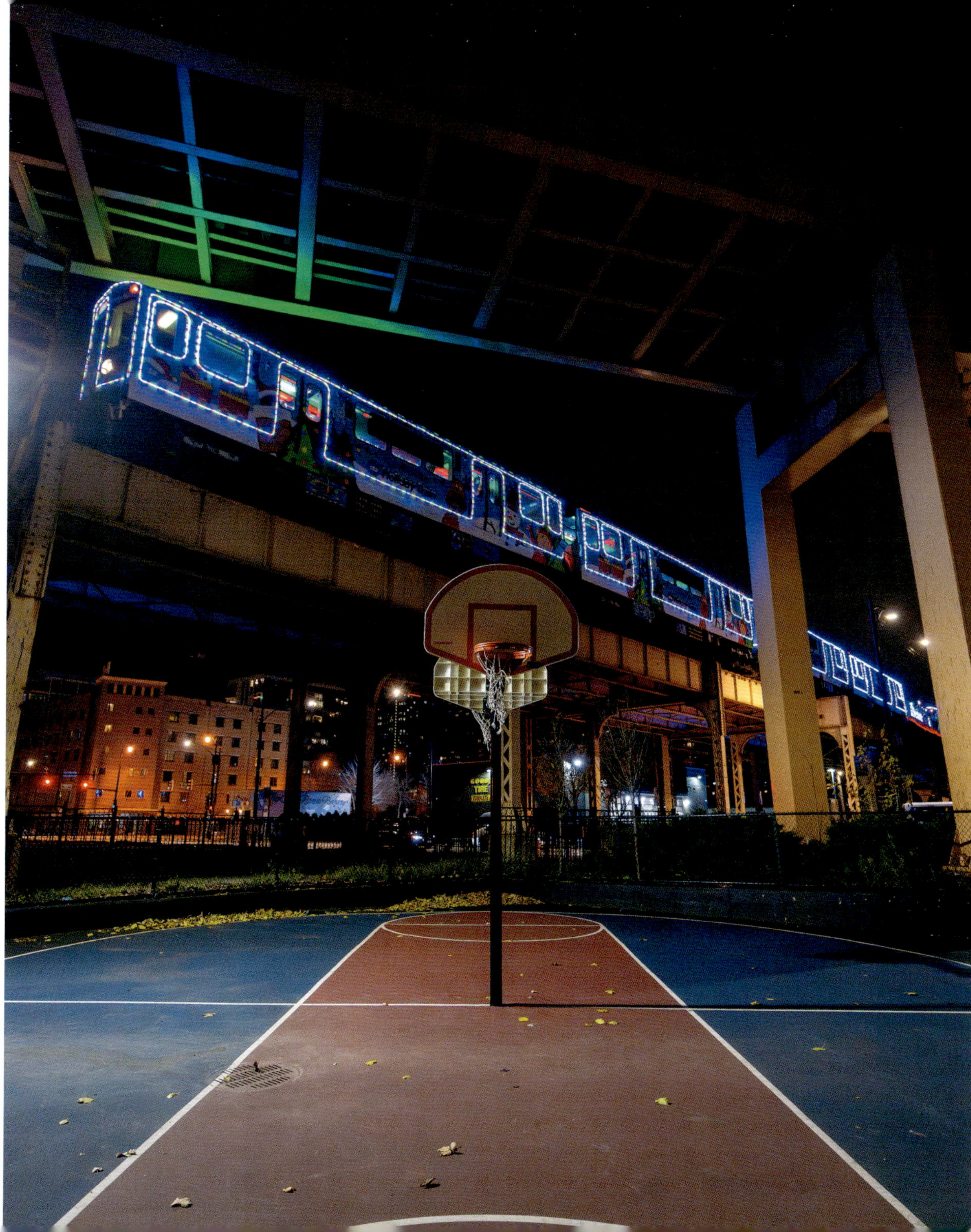

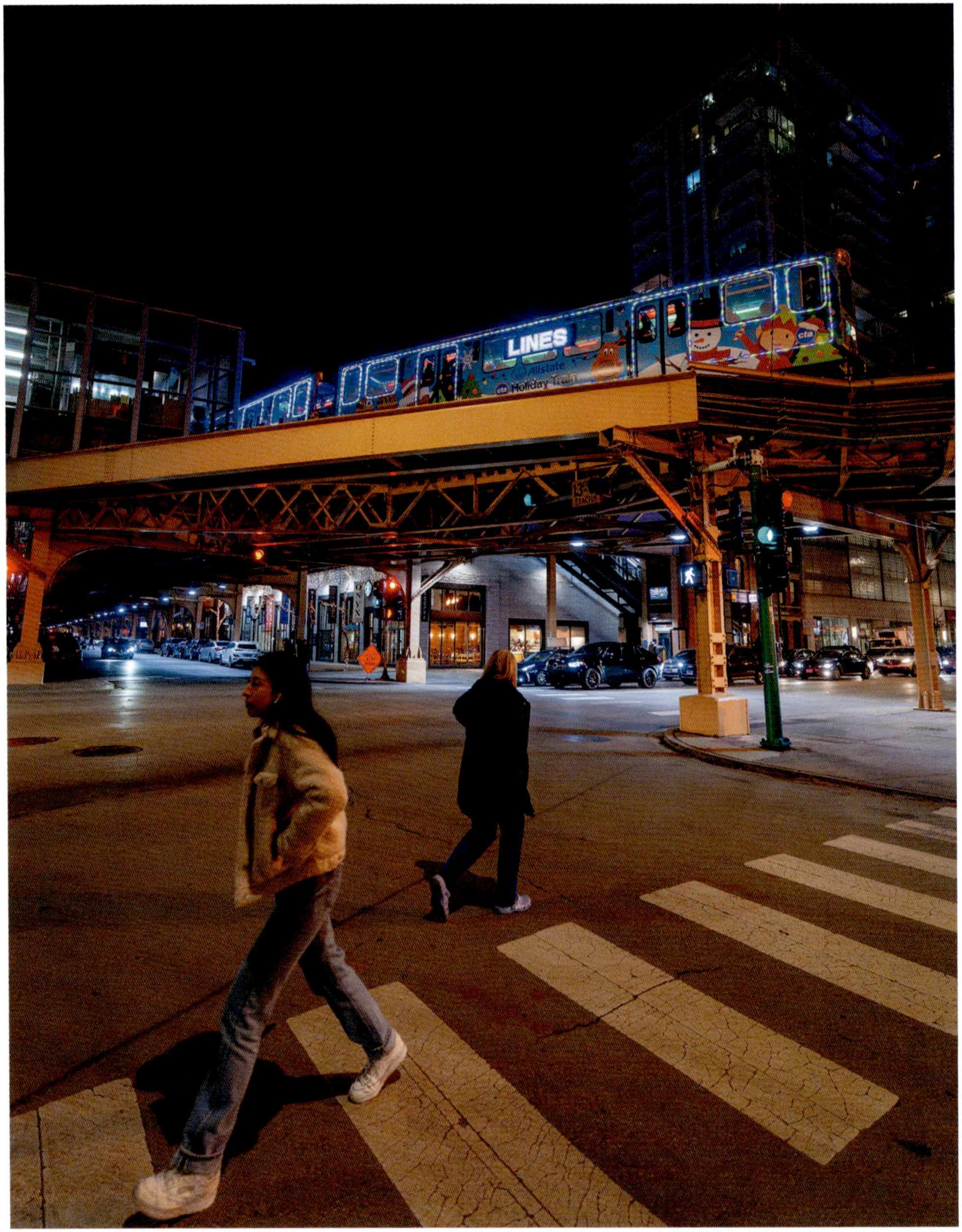

ABOVE: Looking down North Franklin Street **RIGHT:** Looking across West North Avenue

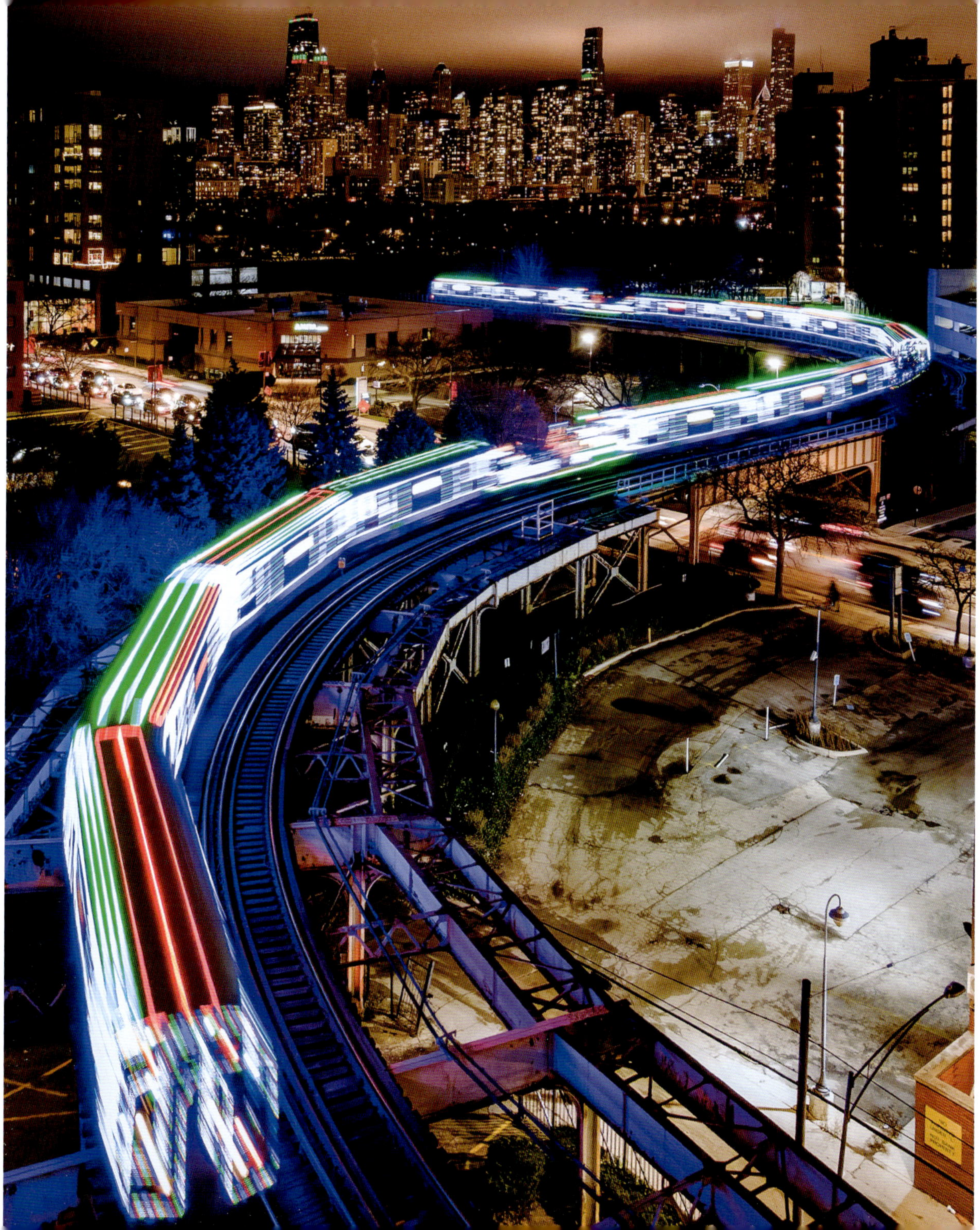

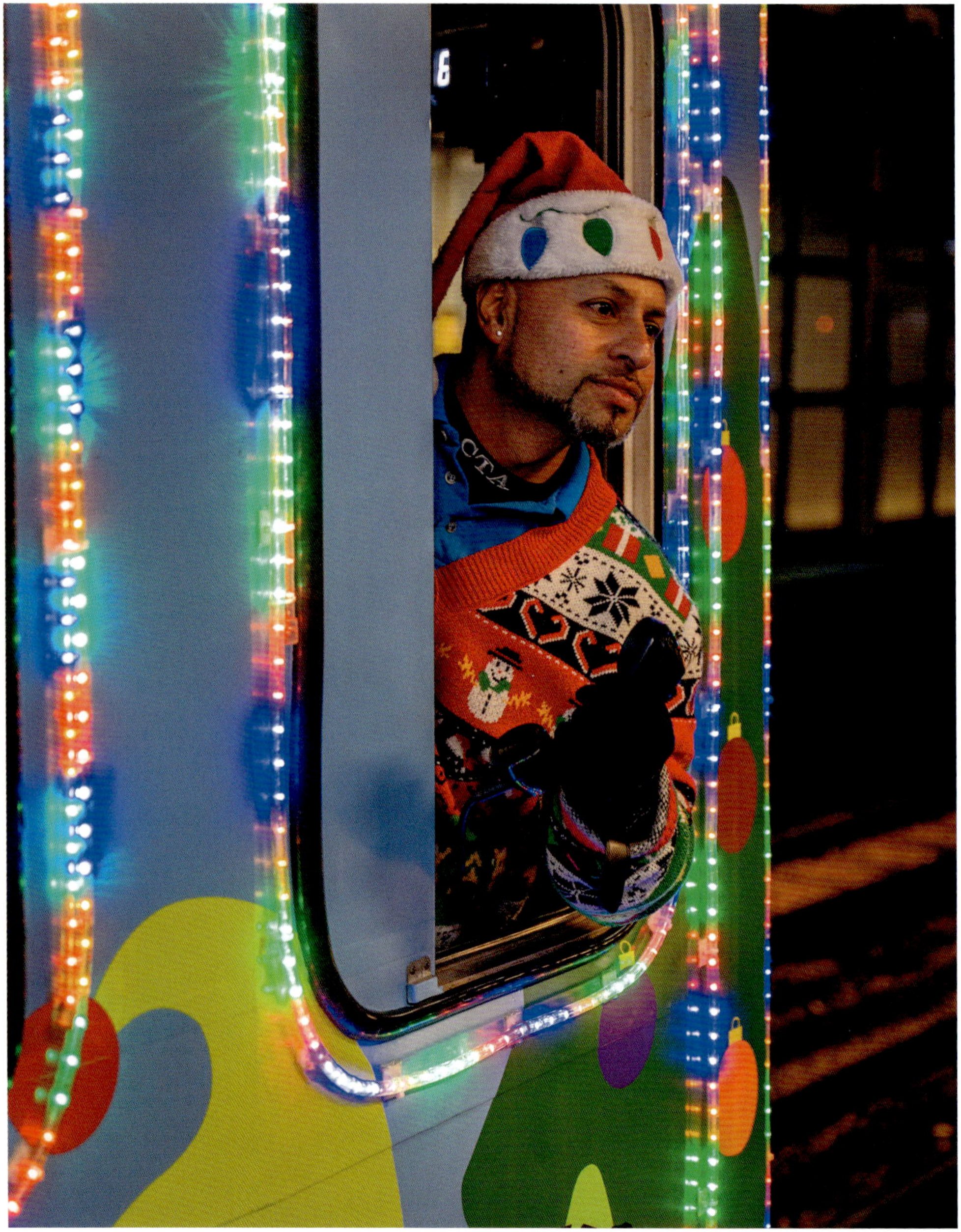

CTA Holiday Train Elf

E'L'ves ride the Holiday Train along with Santa, bringing cheer to all the riders throughout the season.

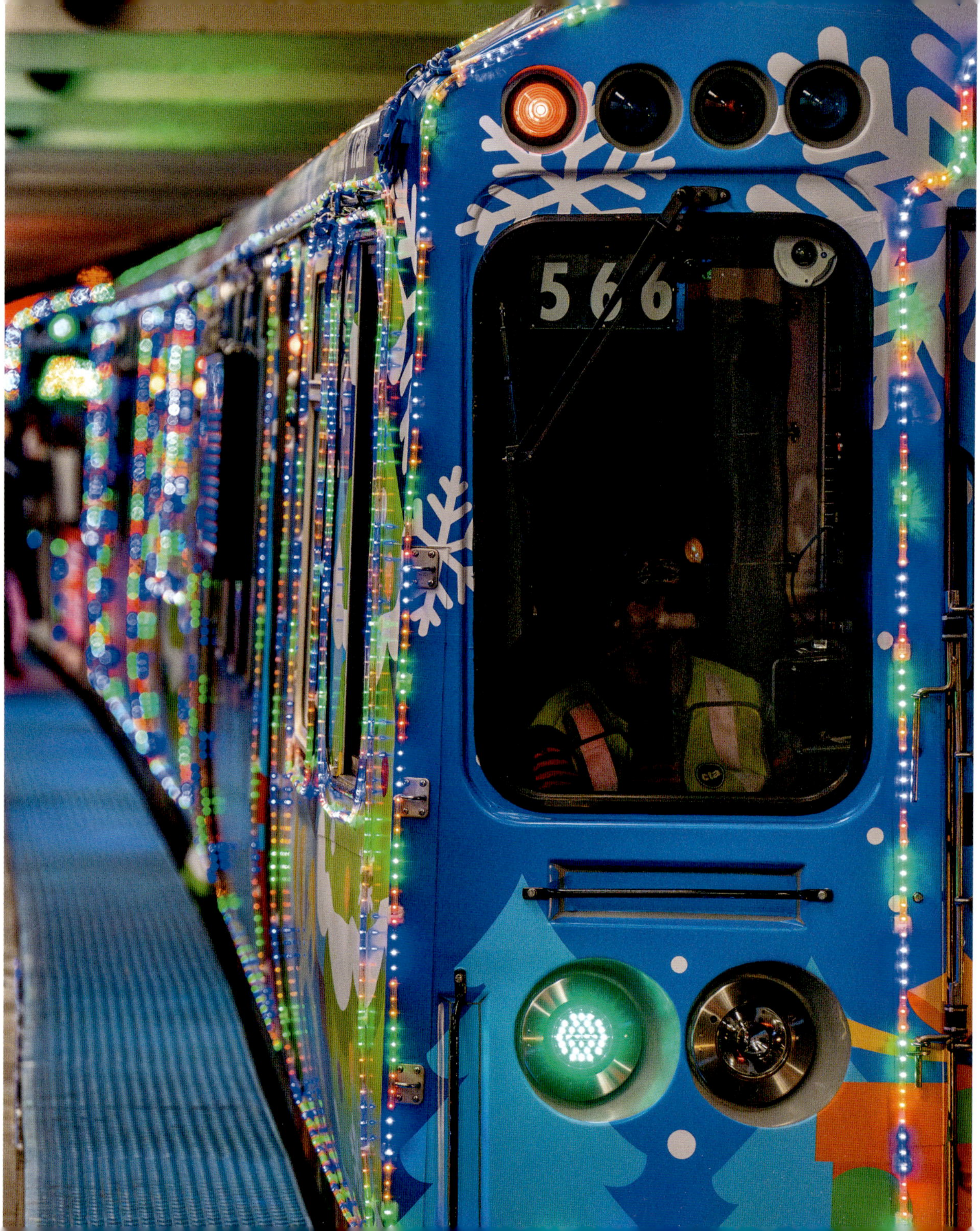
566

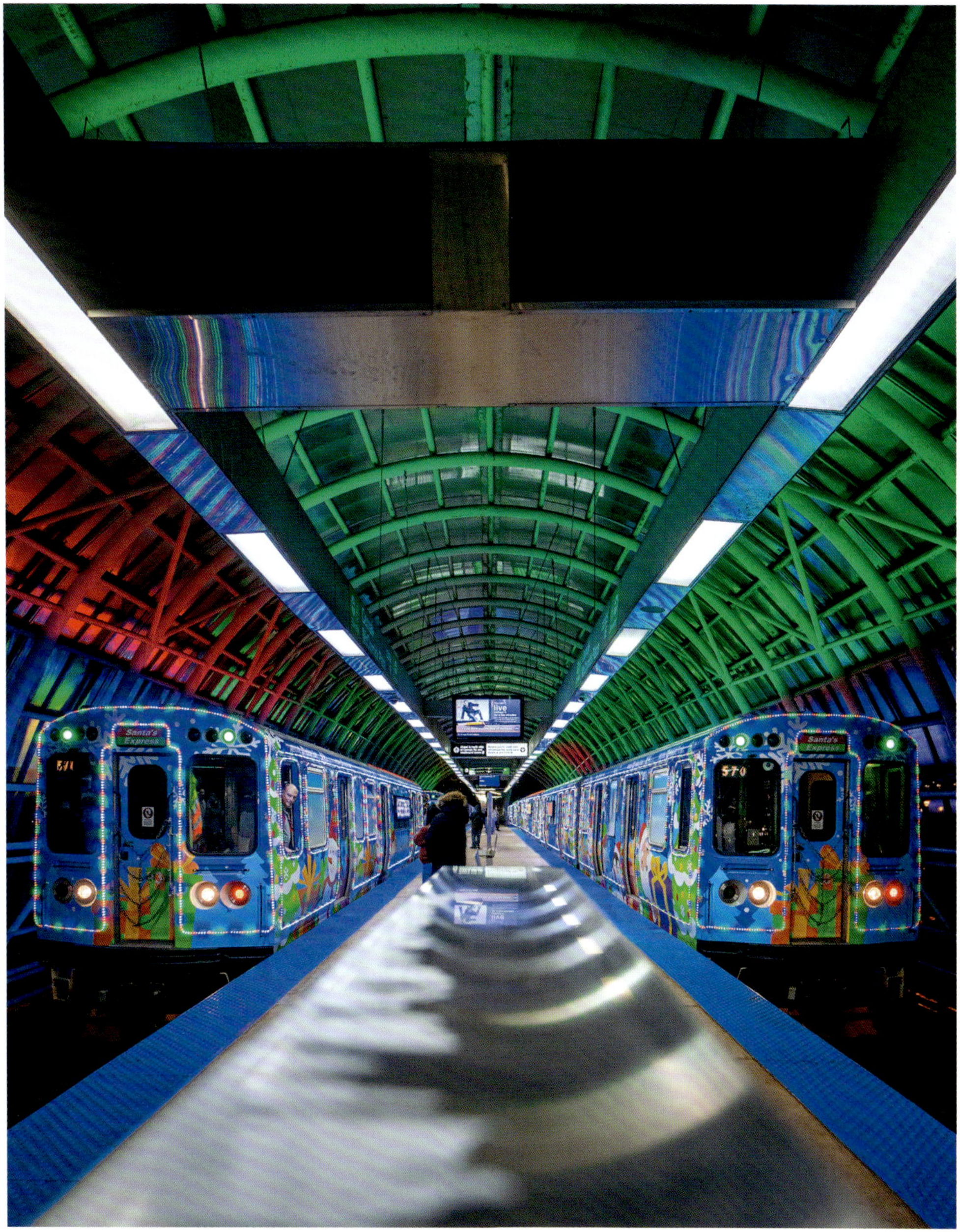

LEFT: CTA Holiday Train Conductor **ABOVE:** Inside Cermak-McCormick Place station

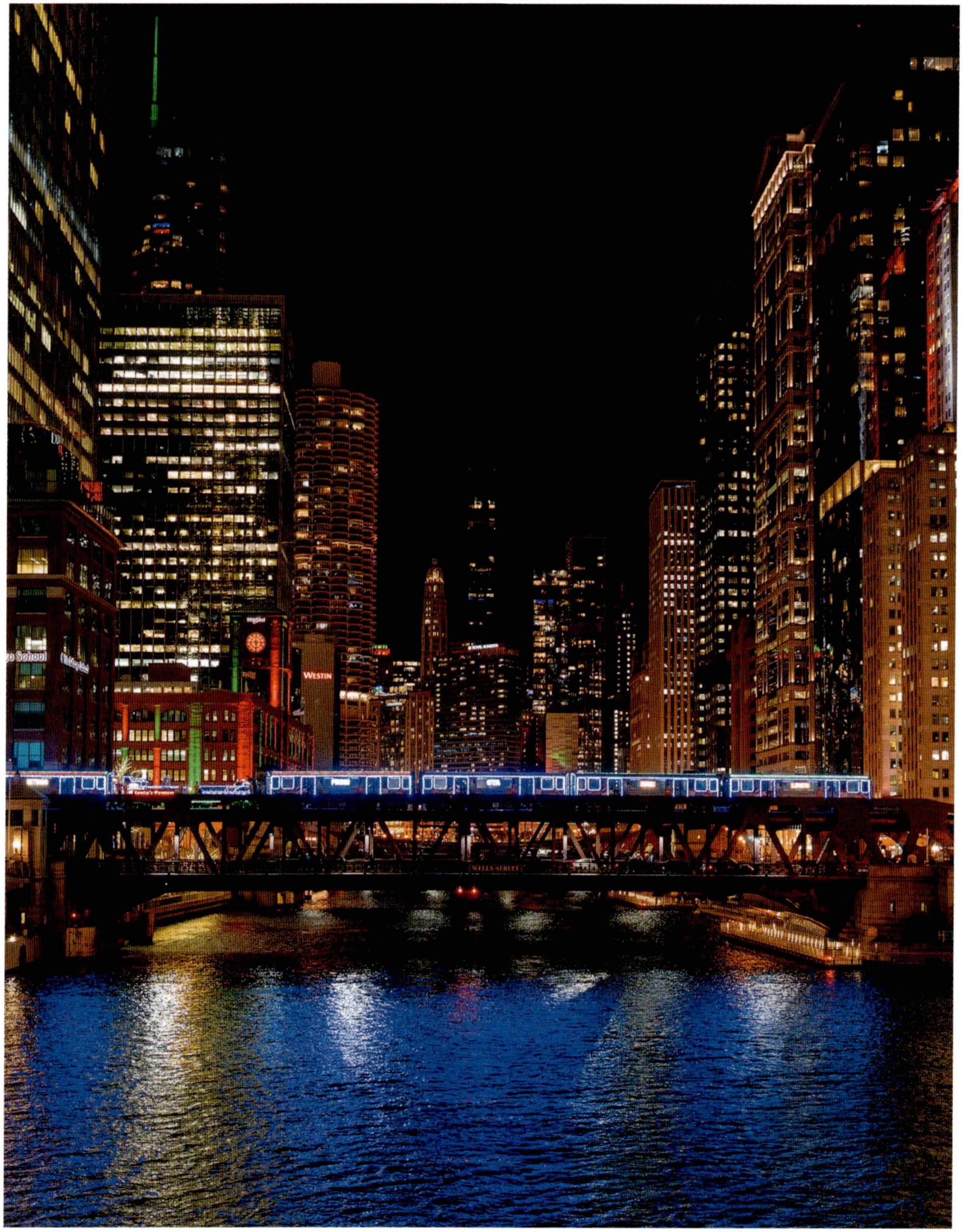

ABOVE: View of Franklin-Orleans Street Bridge **RIGHT:** Above North Wells Street and West Hubbard Street

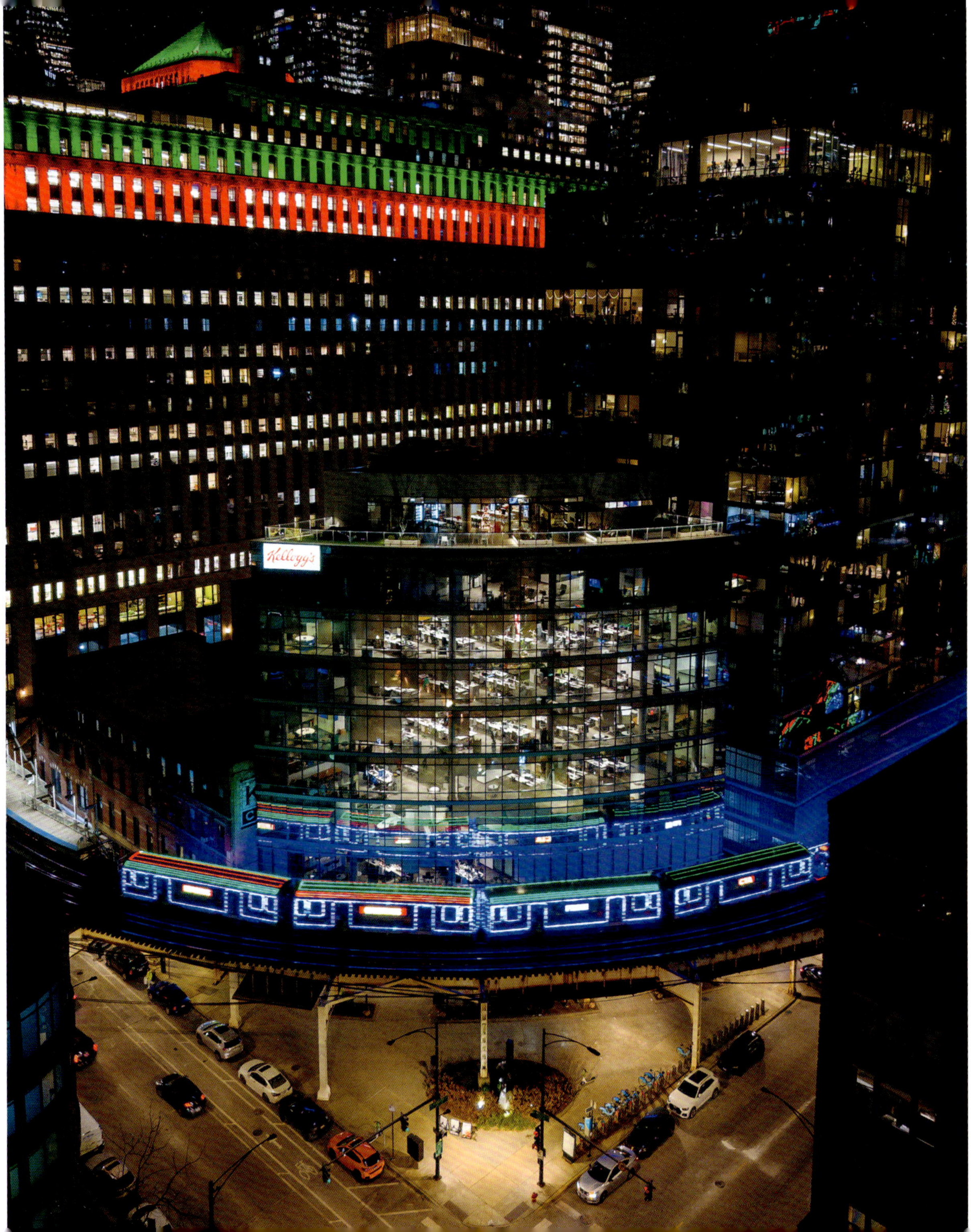
Kellogg's

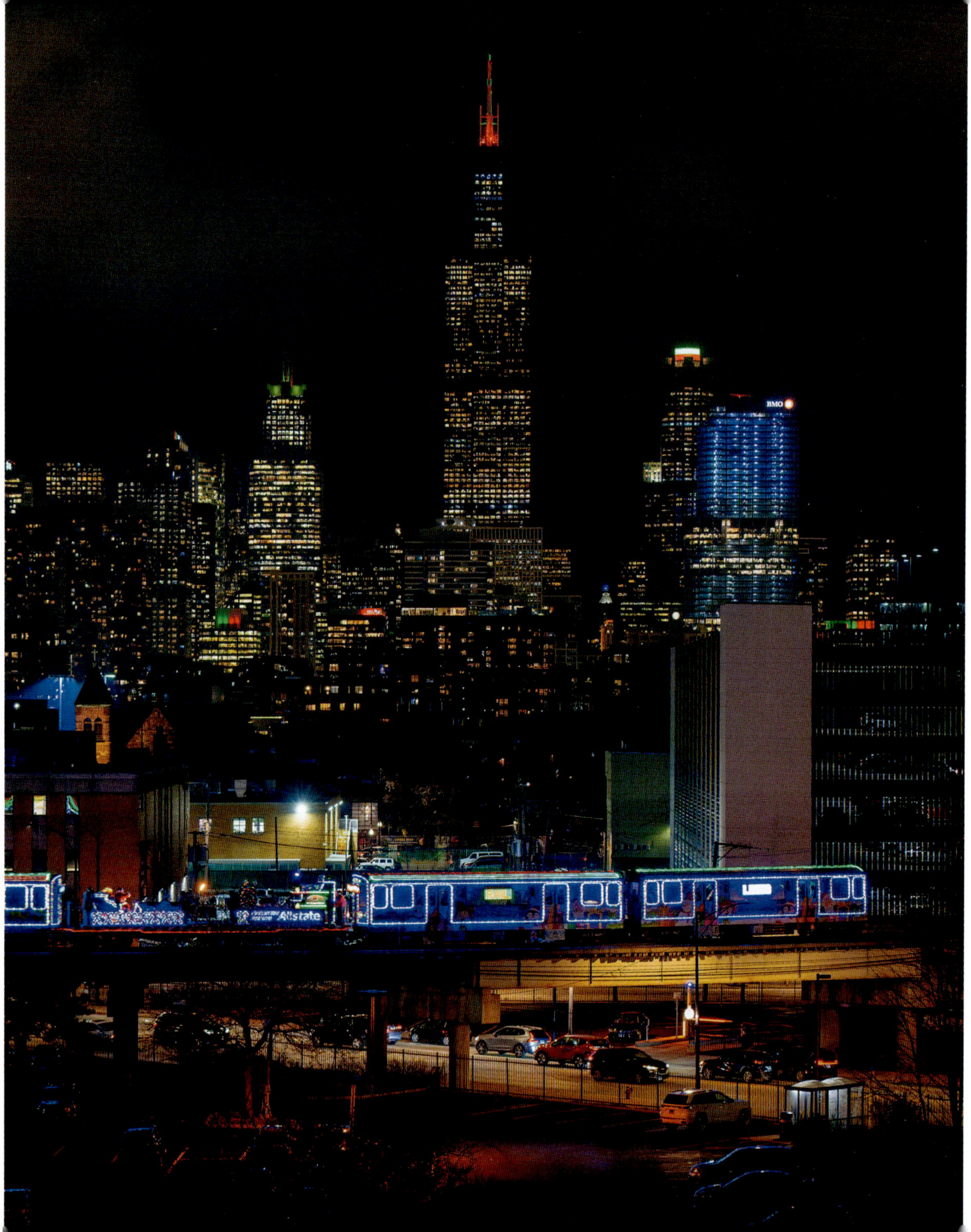
BMO
Allstate

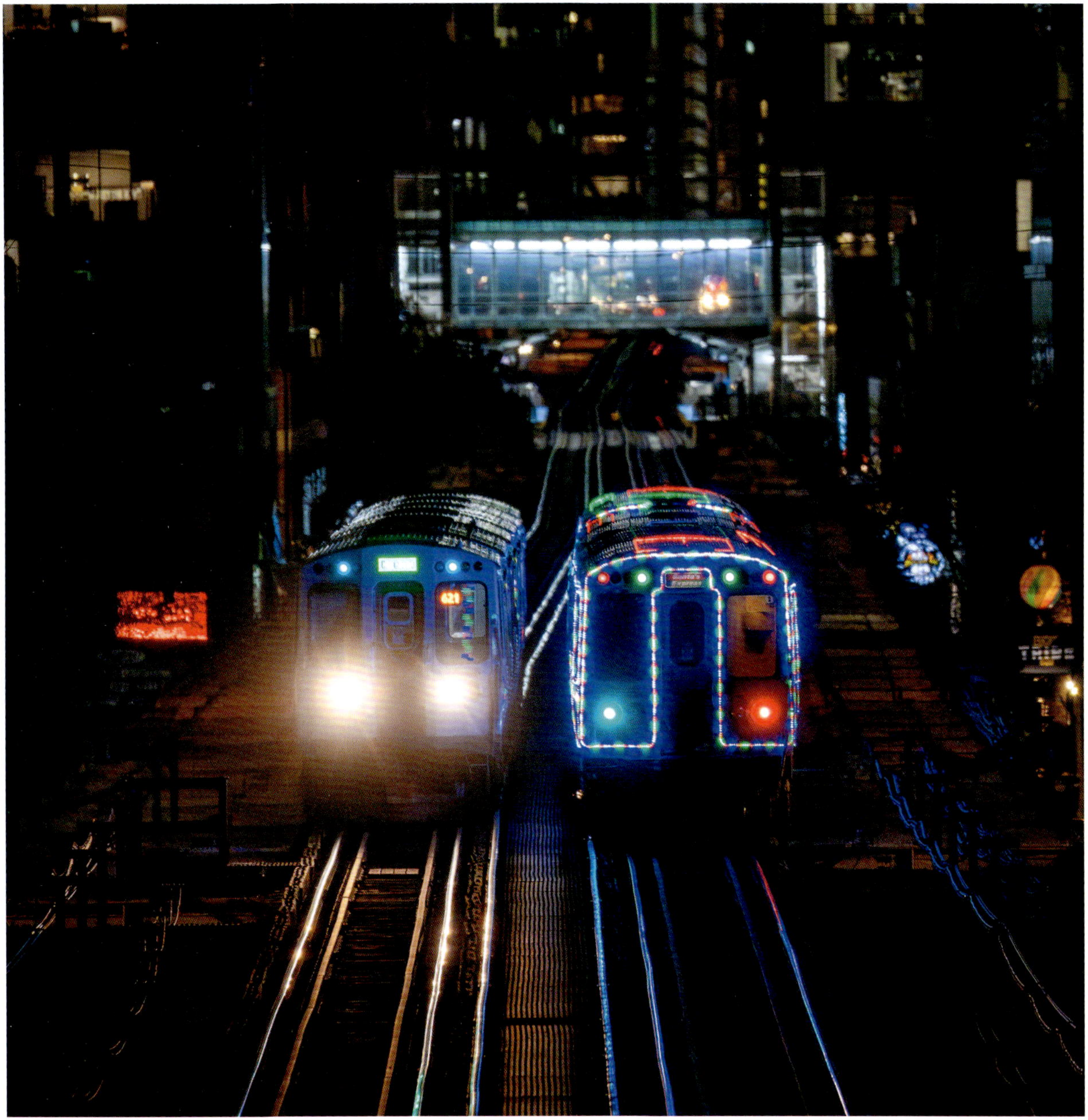

LEFT: Skyline view from the United Center **ABOVE:** Outside the Damen station

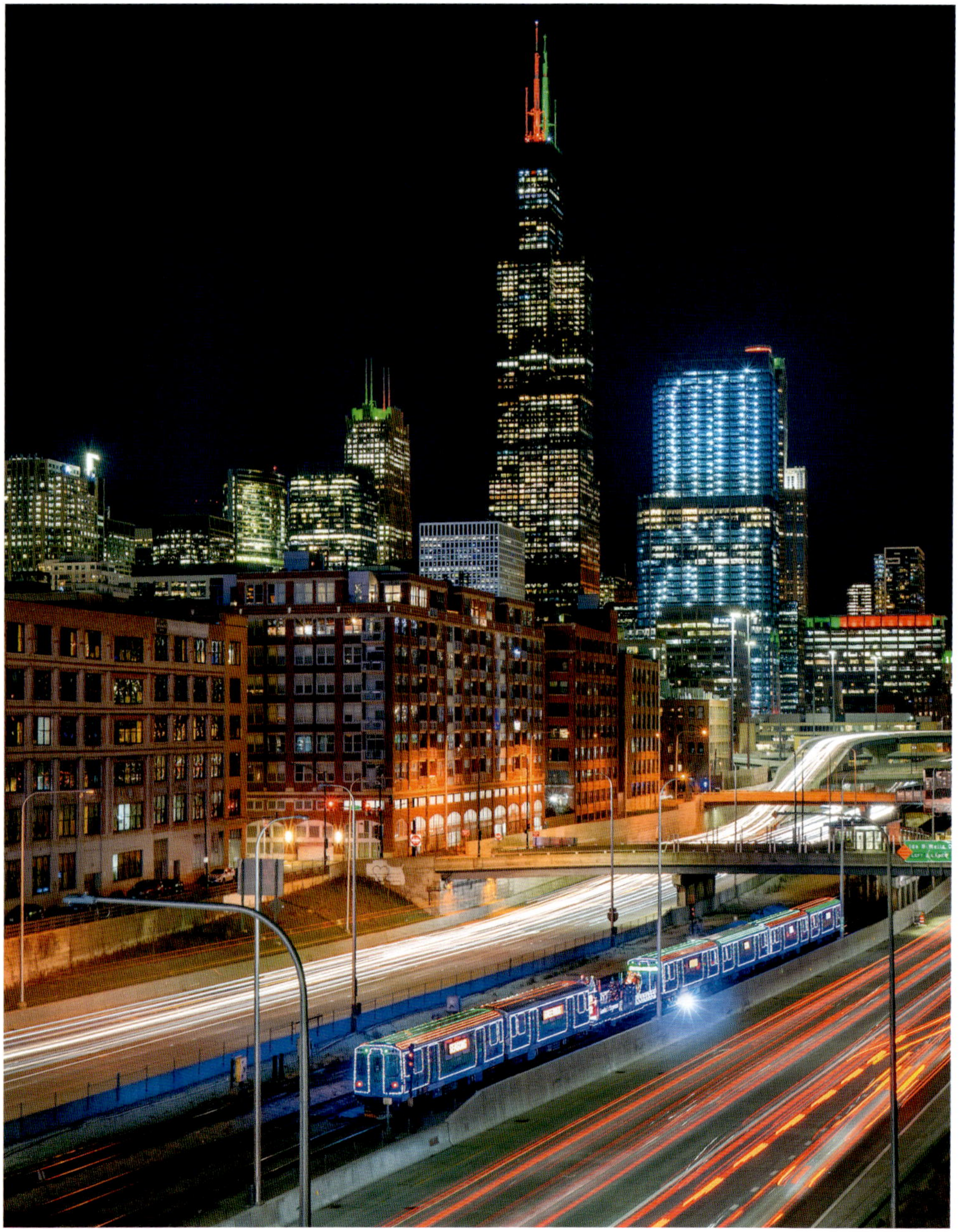

ABOVE: Skyline view from the Racine Street Bridge **RIGHT:** Skyline view from the Paulina Street Bridge

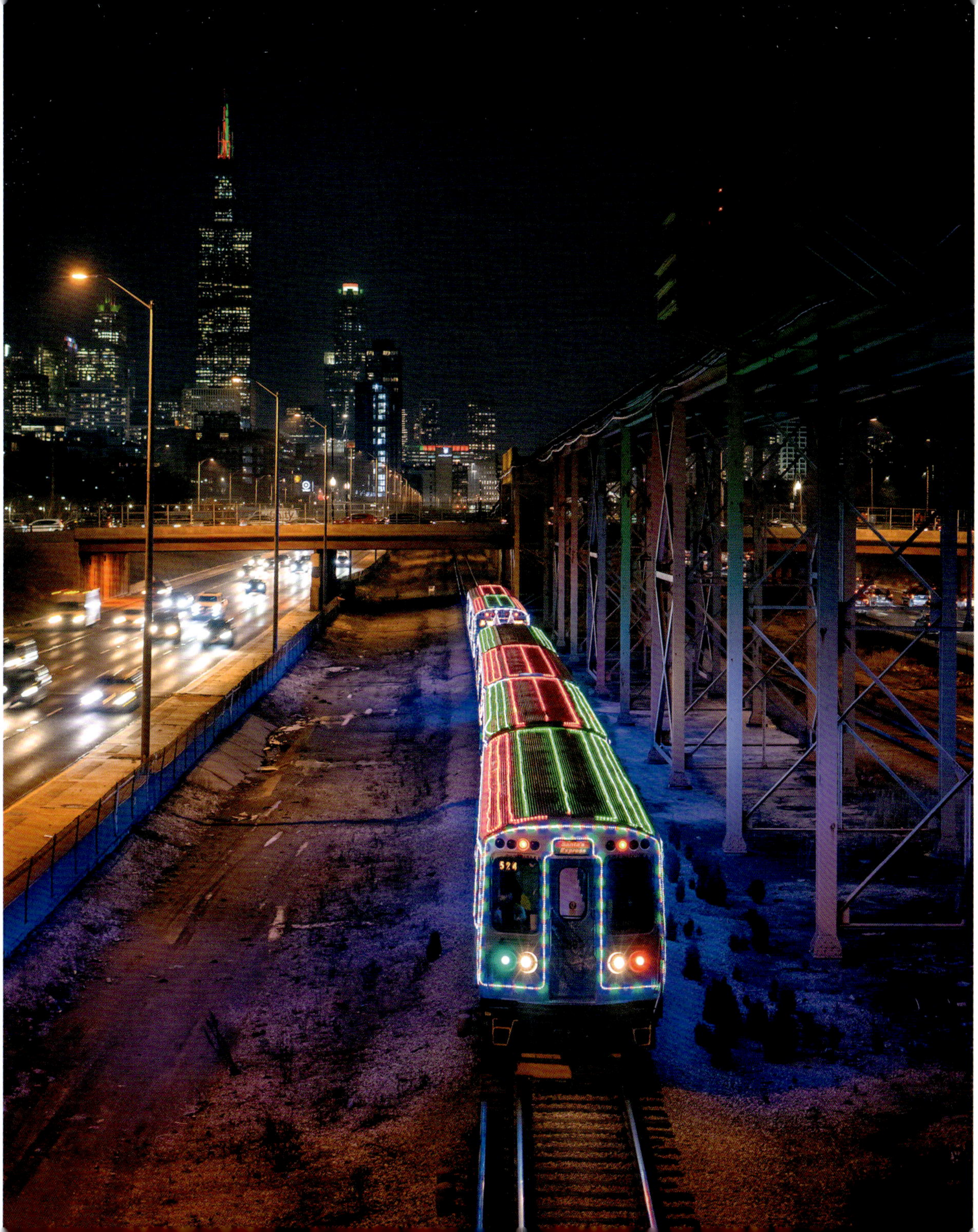
Santa's Express
524

It takes a village. Since 2015, the Holiday Train has had corporate sponsorships to help cover the cost of decorating and running the train each year.

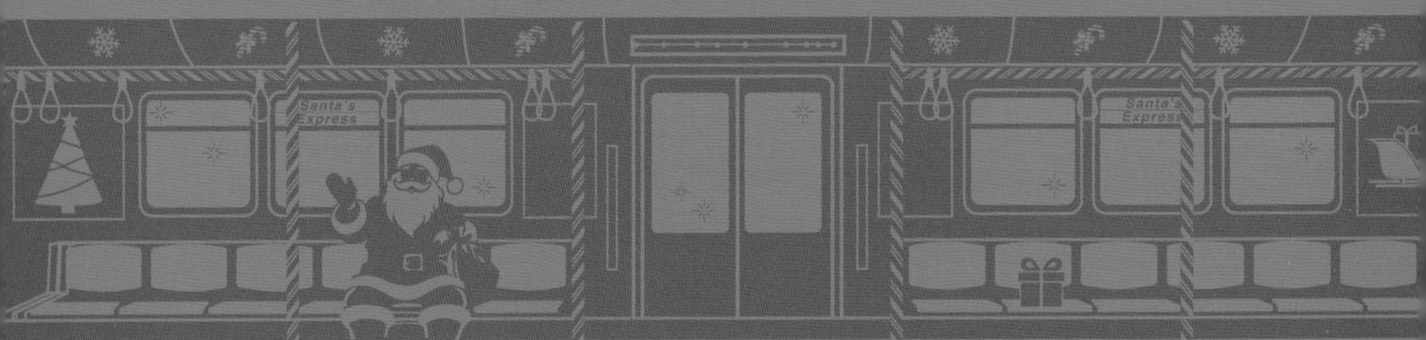

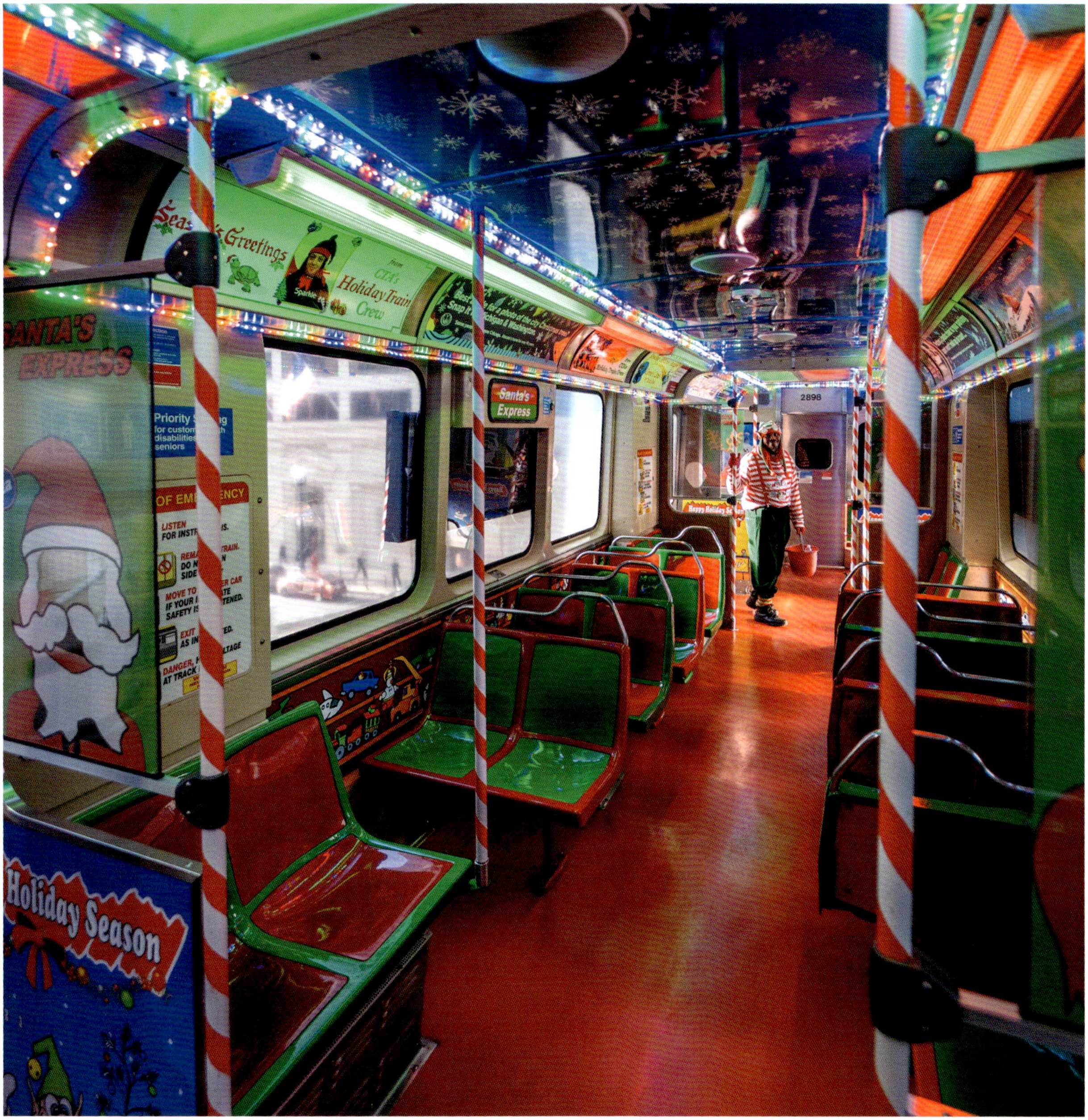

Inside the CTA Holiday Train

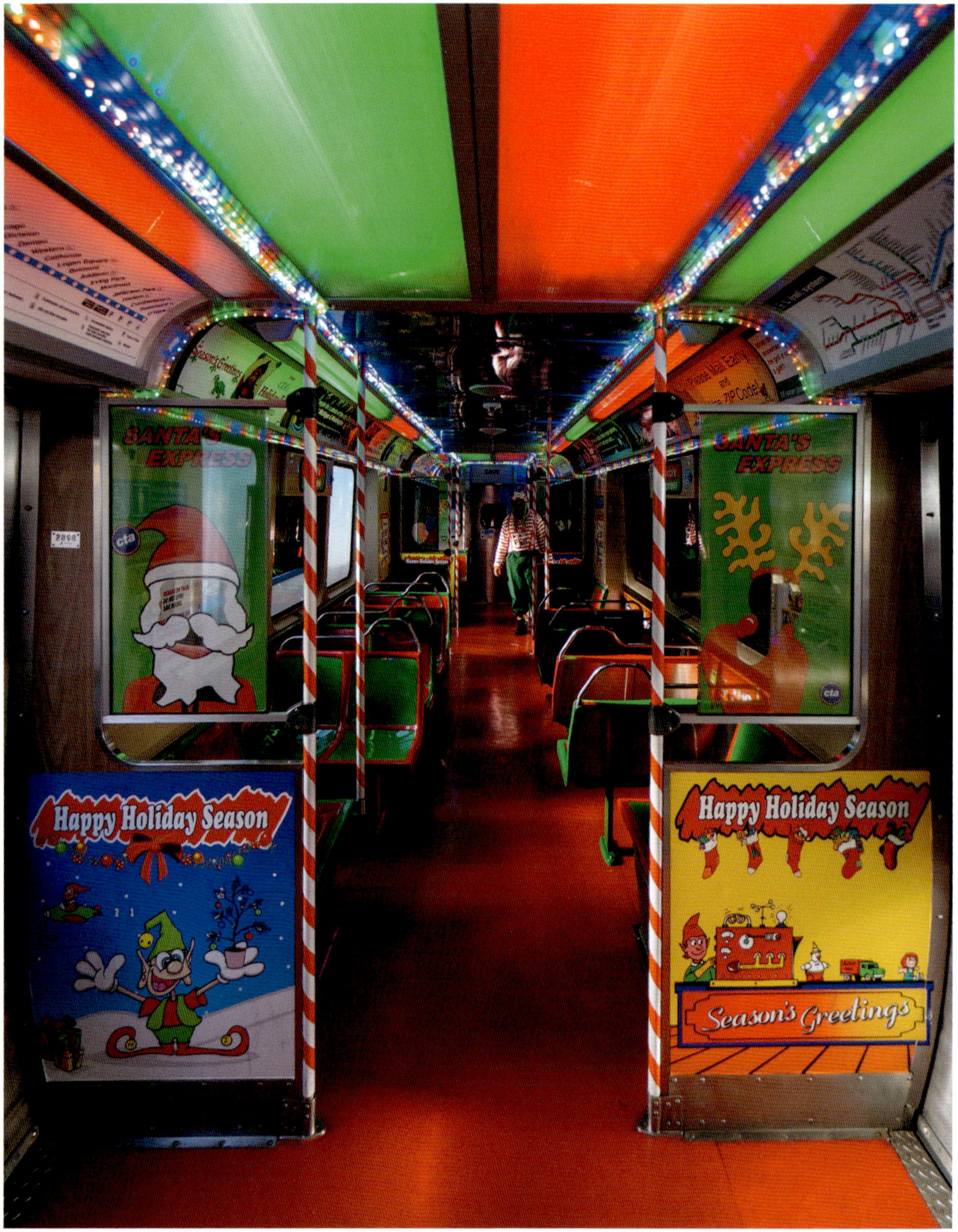

ABOVE & RIGHT: Inside the CTA Holiday Train

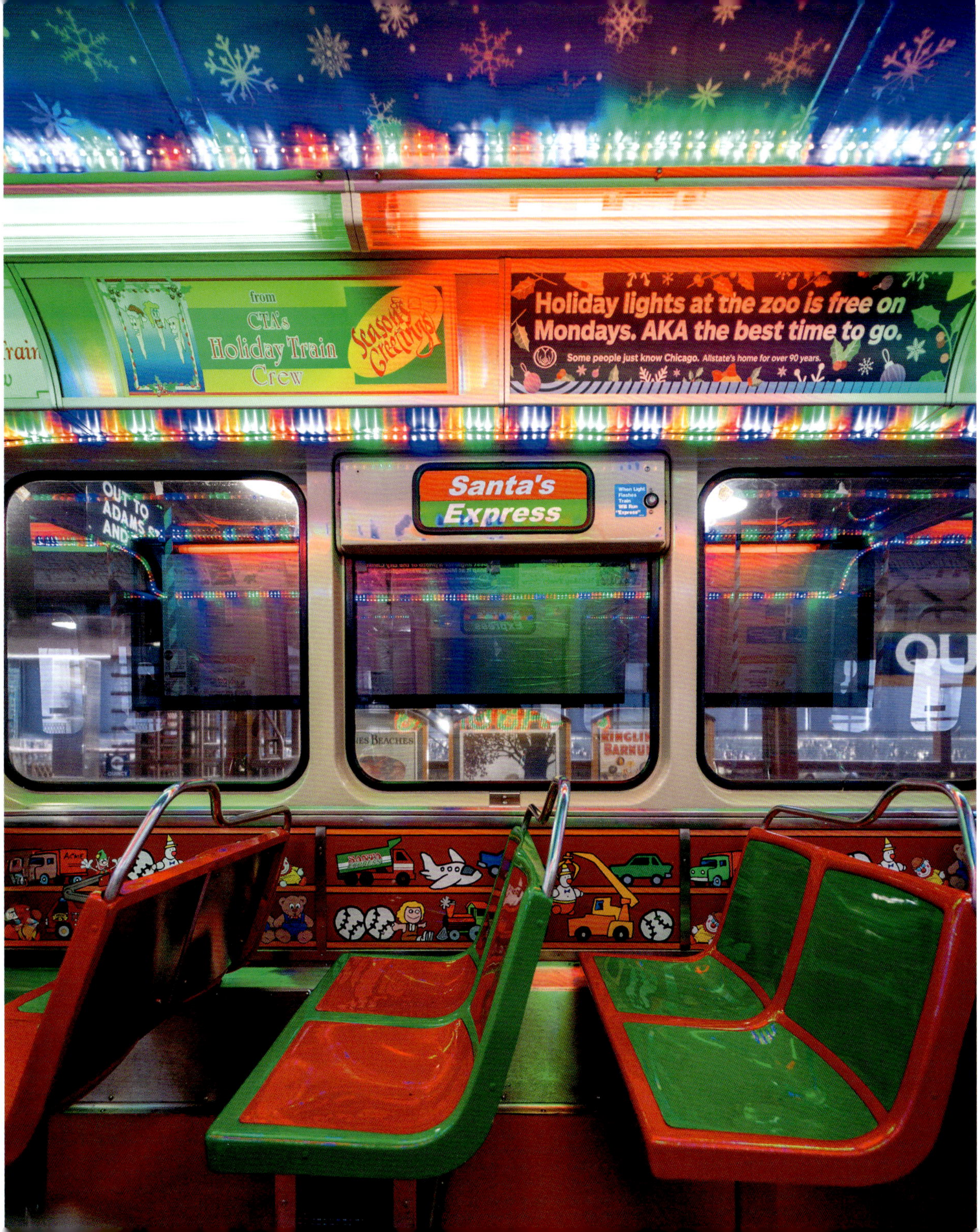
from
CTA's
Holiday Train
Crew
Season's Greetings
Holiday lights at the zoo is free on
Mondays. AKA the best time to go.
Some people just know Chicago. Allstate's home for over 90 years.
Santa's
Express

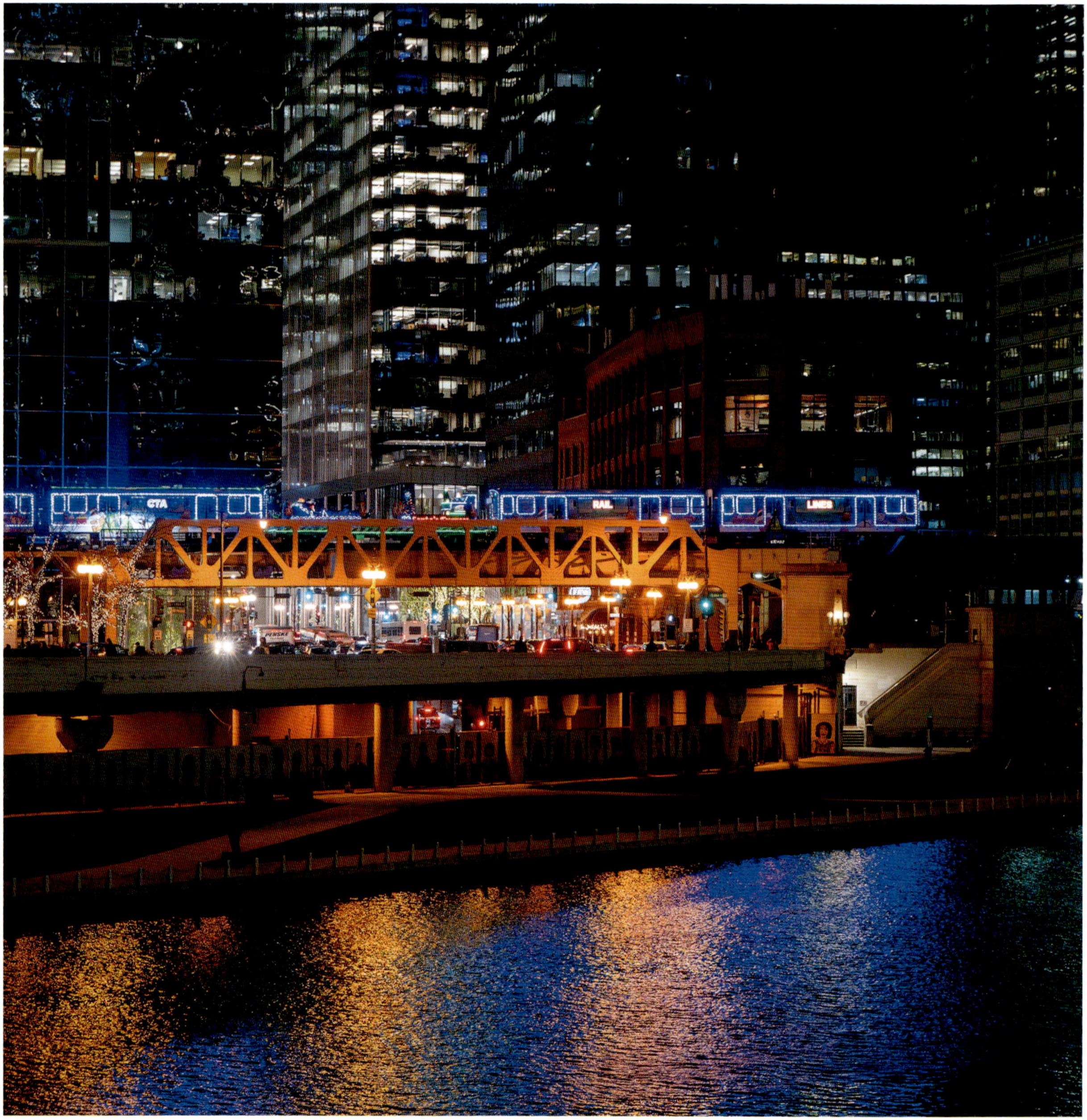
CTA
RAIL
LINES

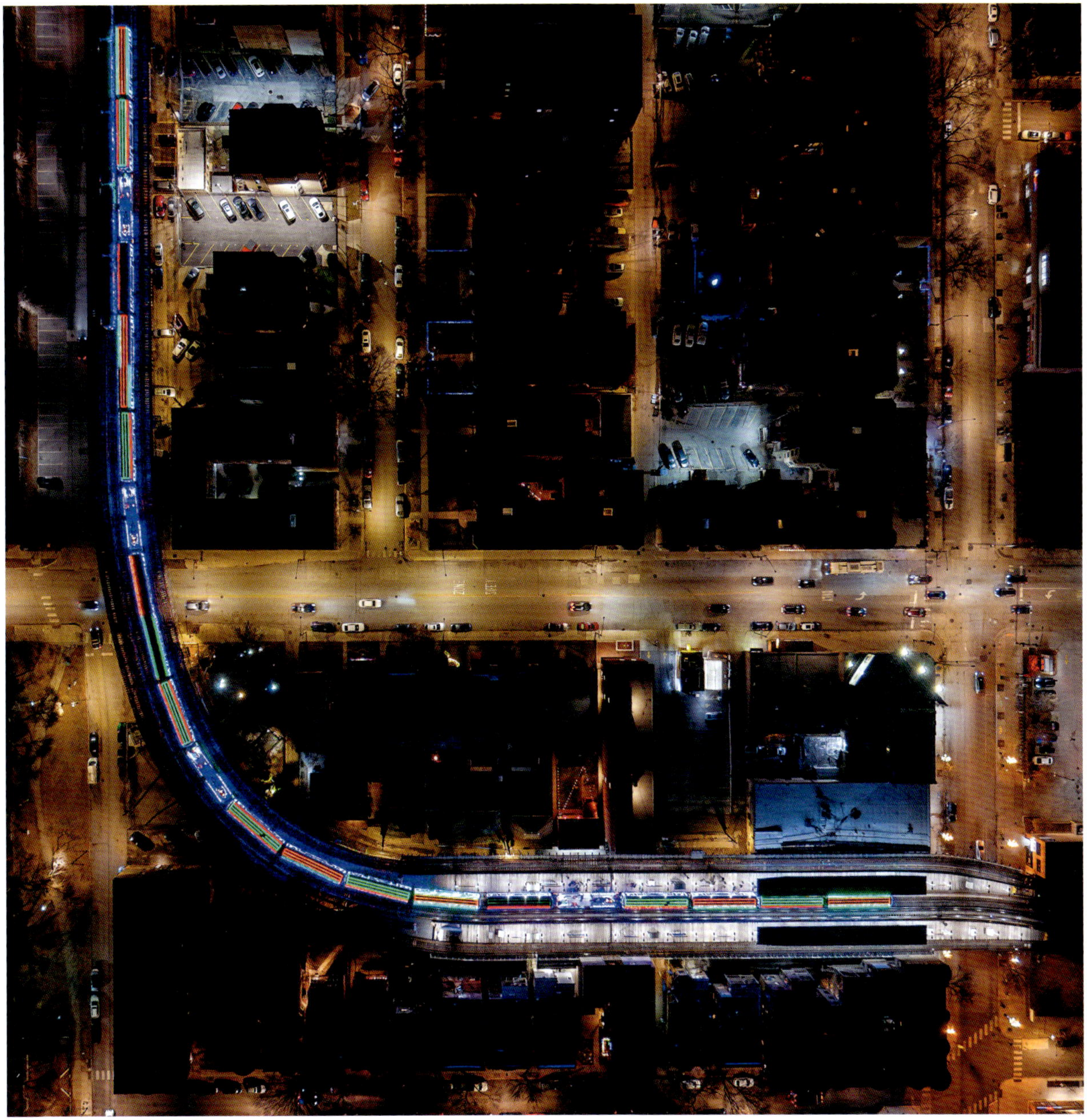

Above the Sheridan station

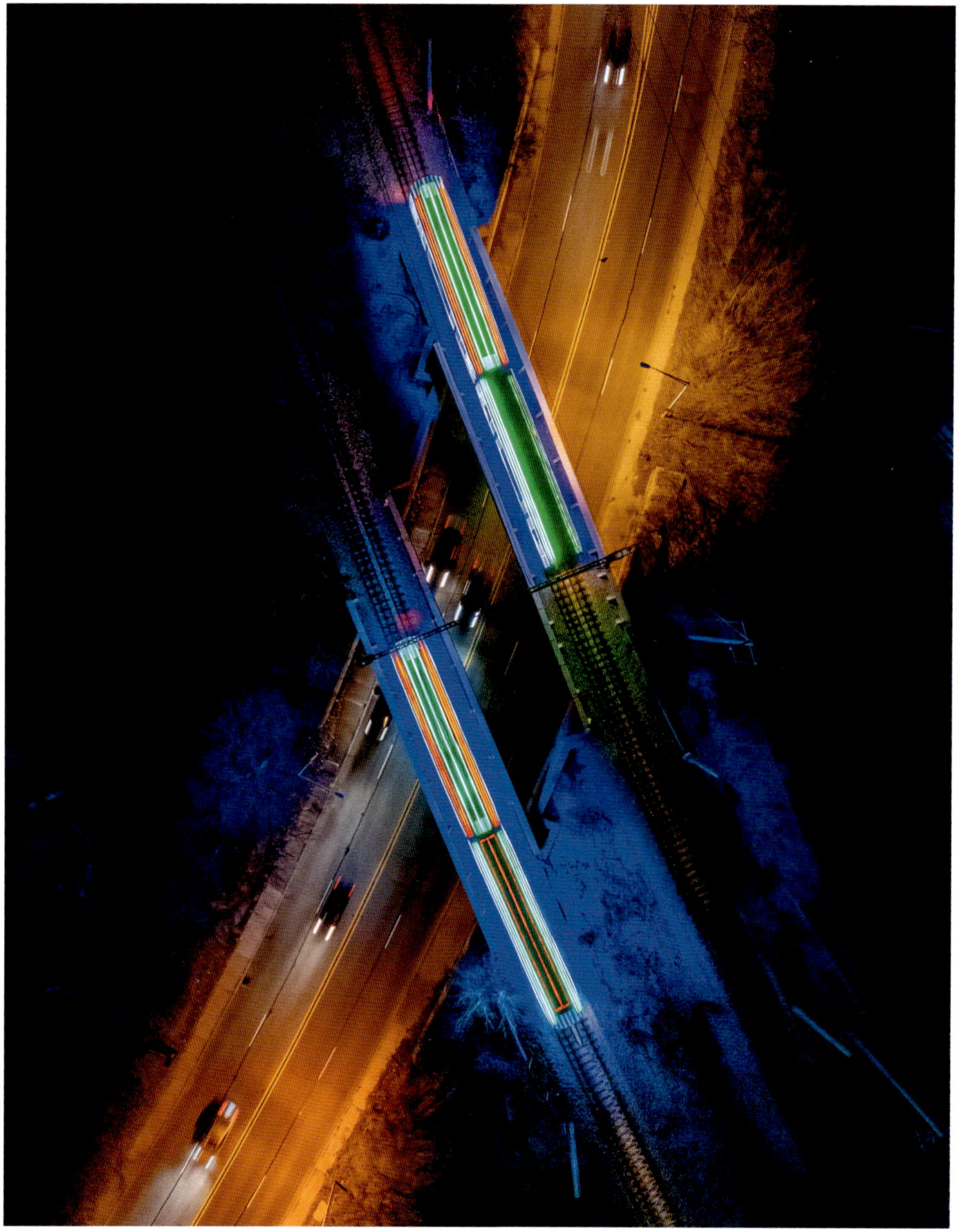

ABOVE: Over Skokie Boulevard **RIGHT:** Above West North Avenue

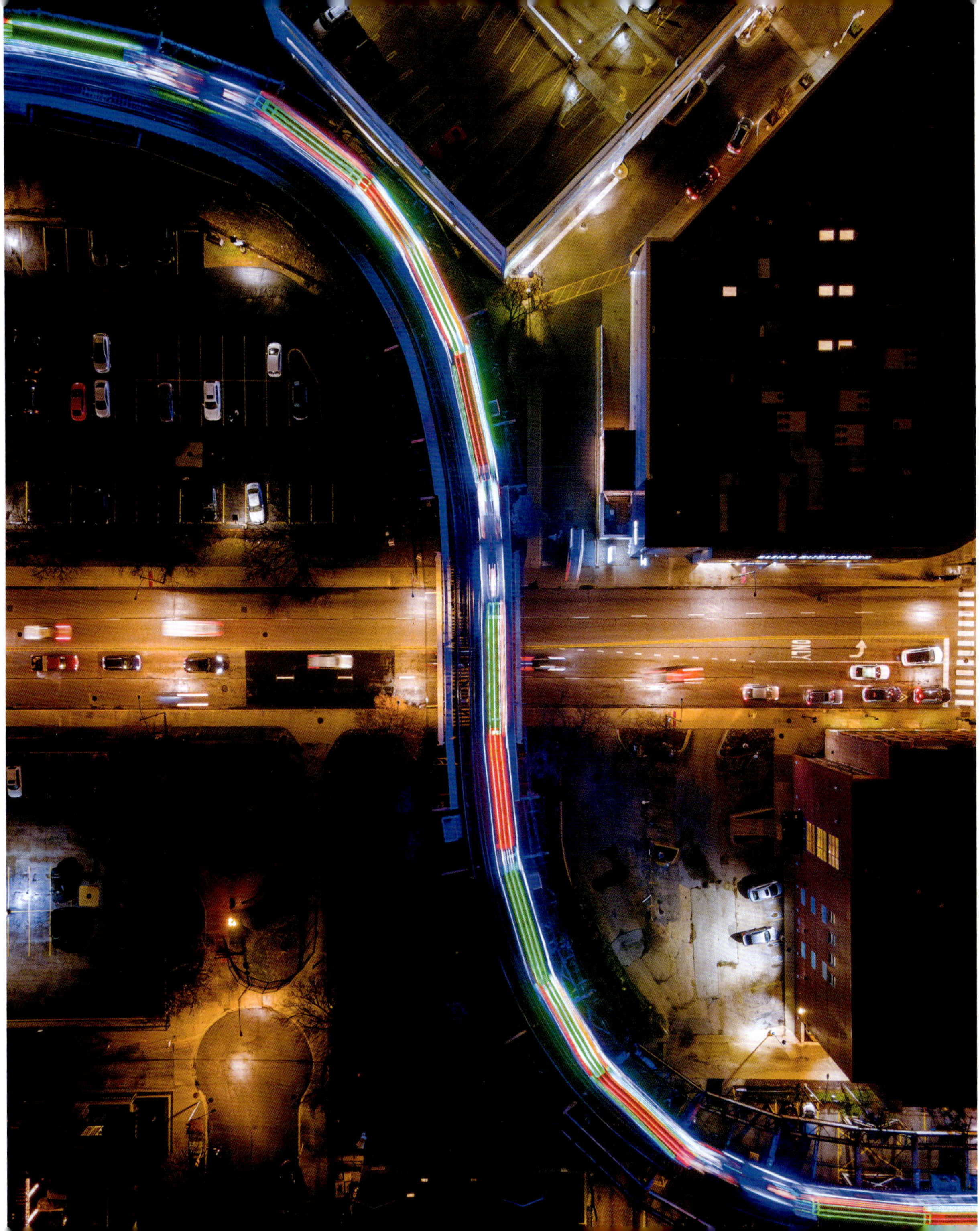
ONLY

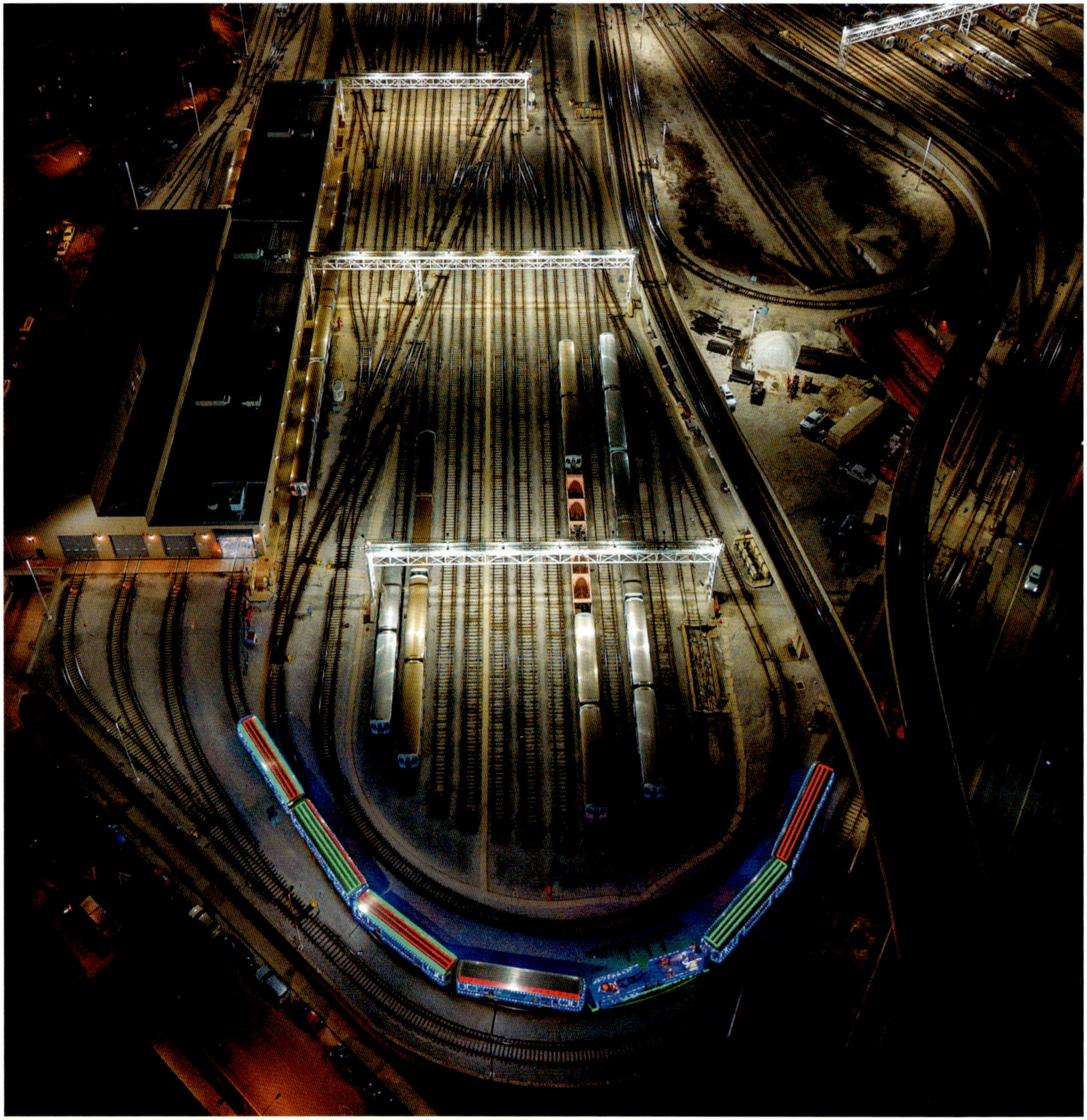

Above Howard CTA Depot

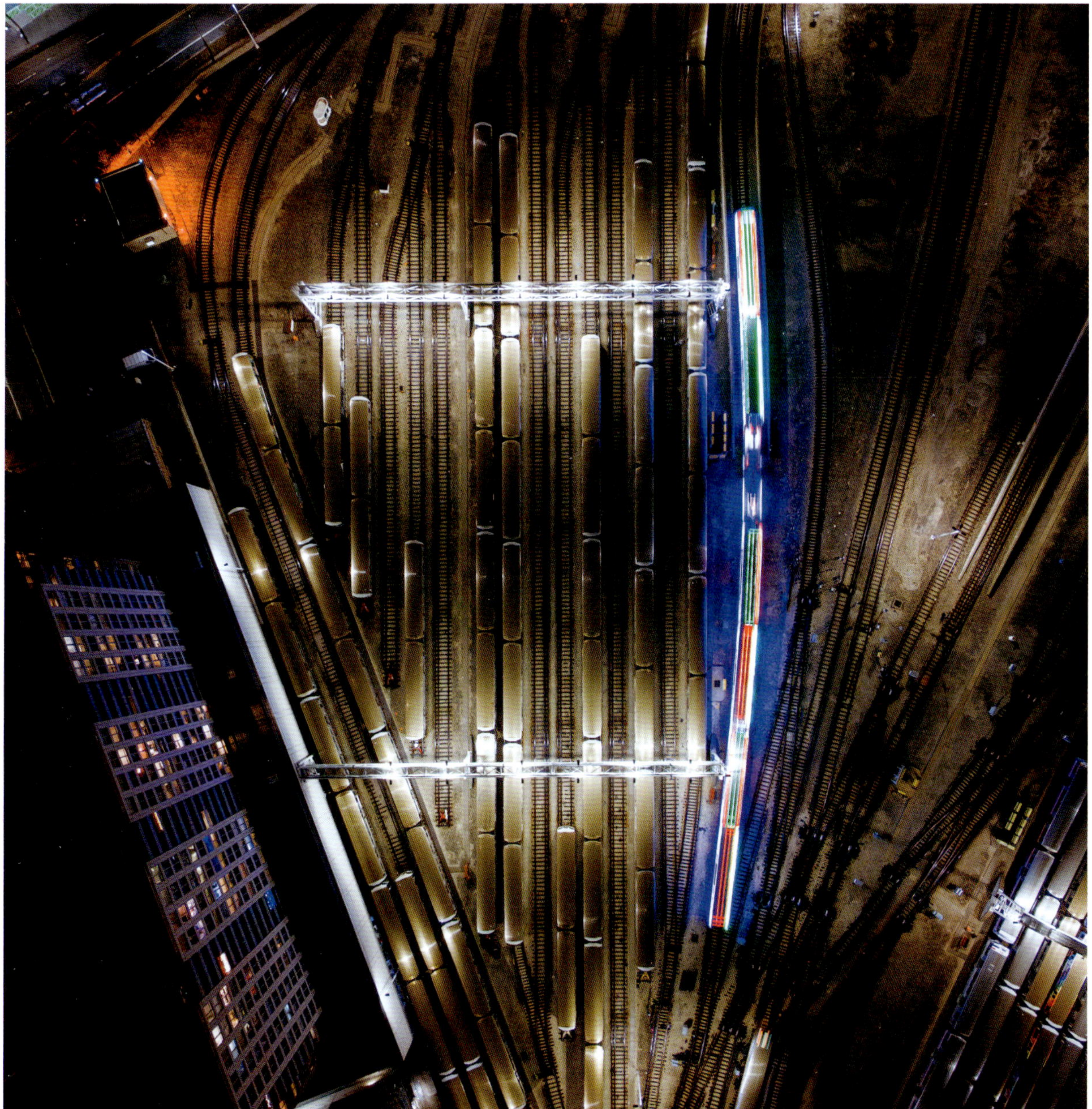

Above Howard CTA Depot

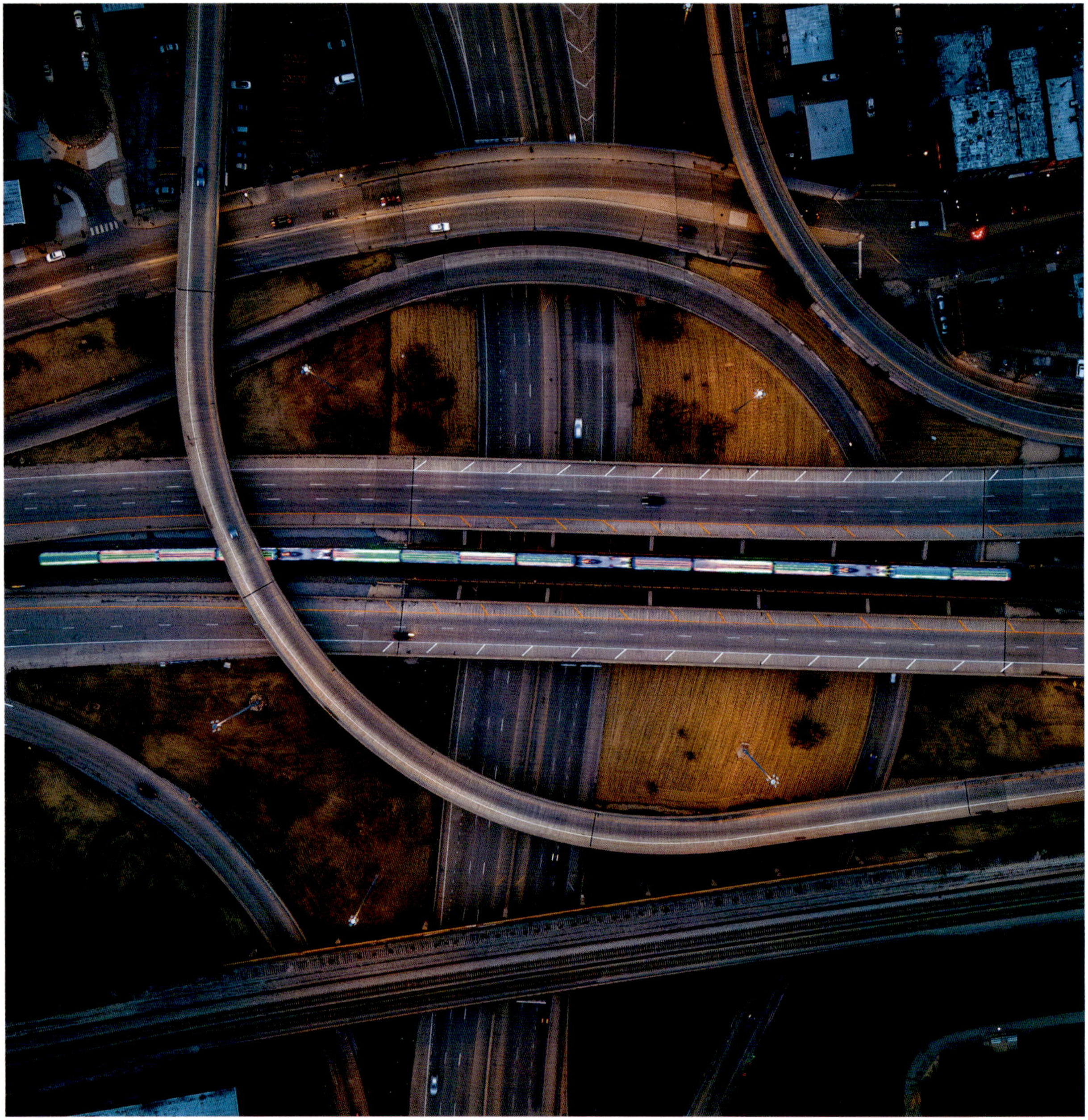

ABOVE: Over the Stevenson Expressway **RIGHT:** Skyline view from 31st Street Bridge

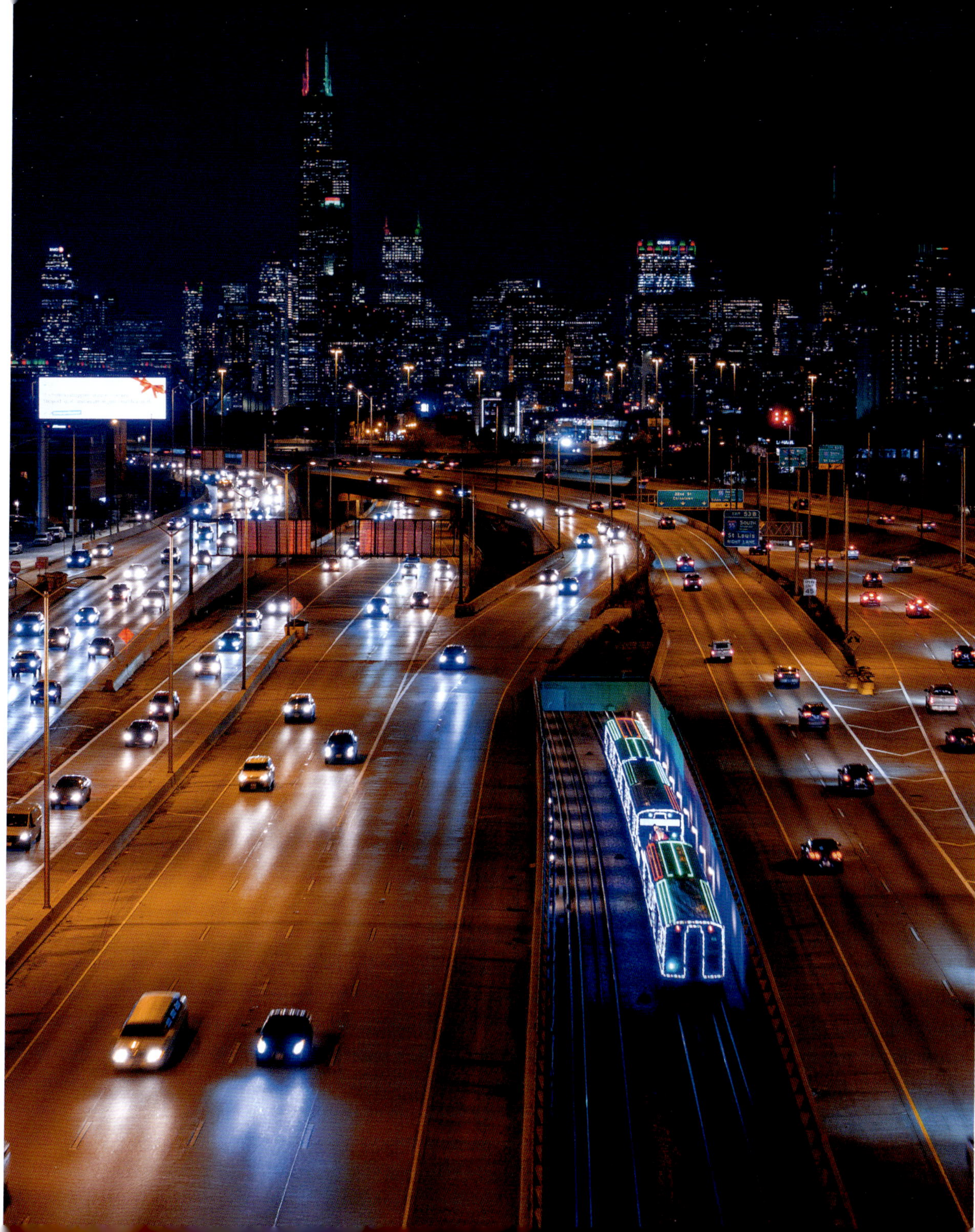
22nd St
Chinatown
53B
South
St Louis
RIGHT LANE
45

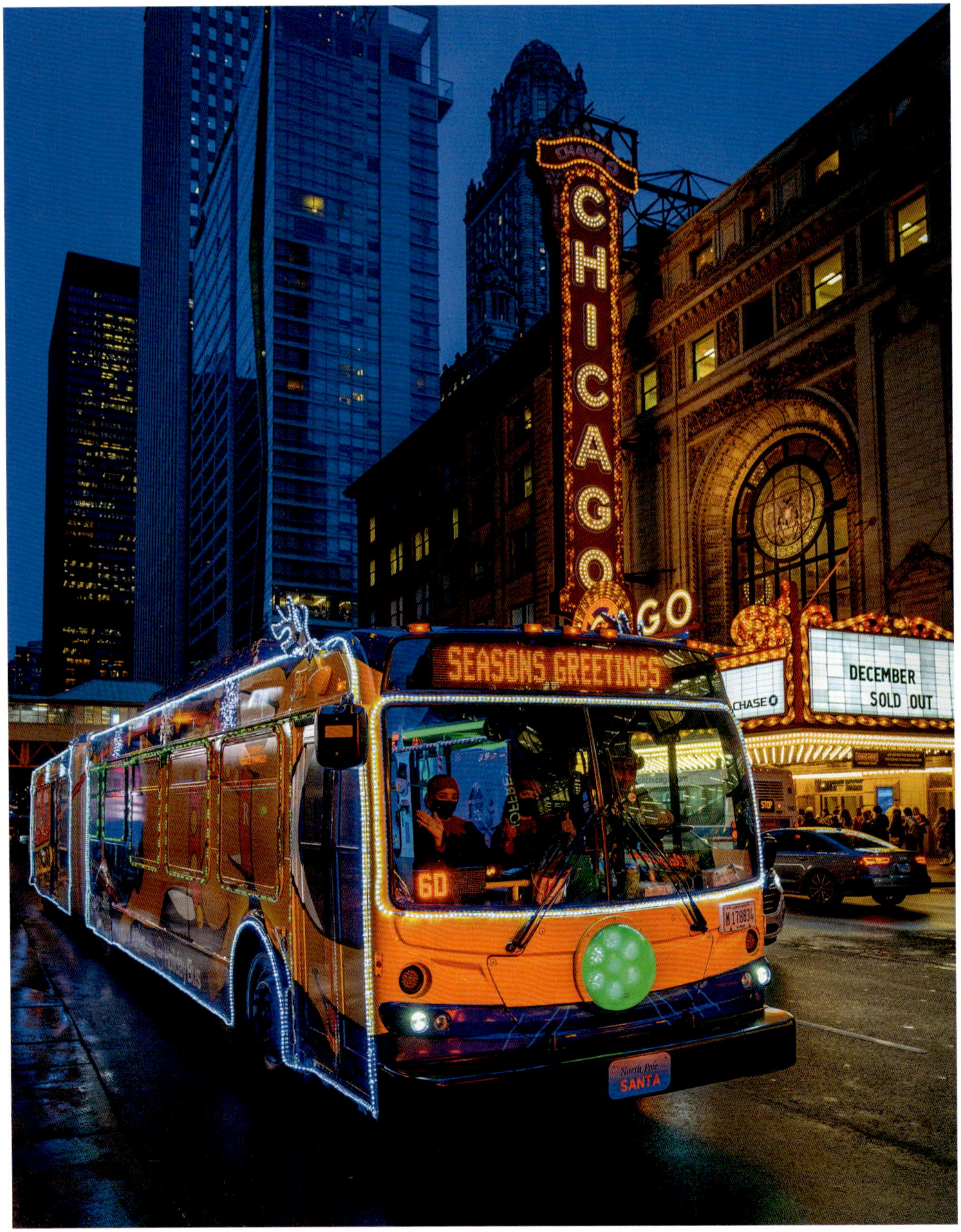

CTA Holiday Bus on North State Street

The Holiday Bus began running in 2014 and now runs on 17 routes across the city of Chicago.

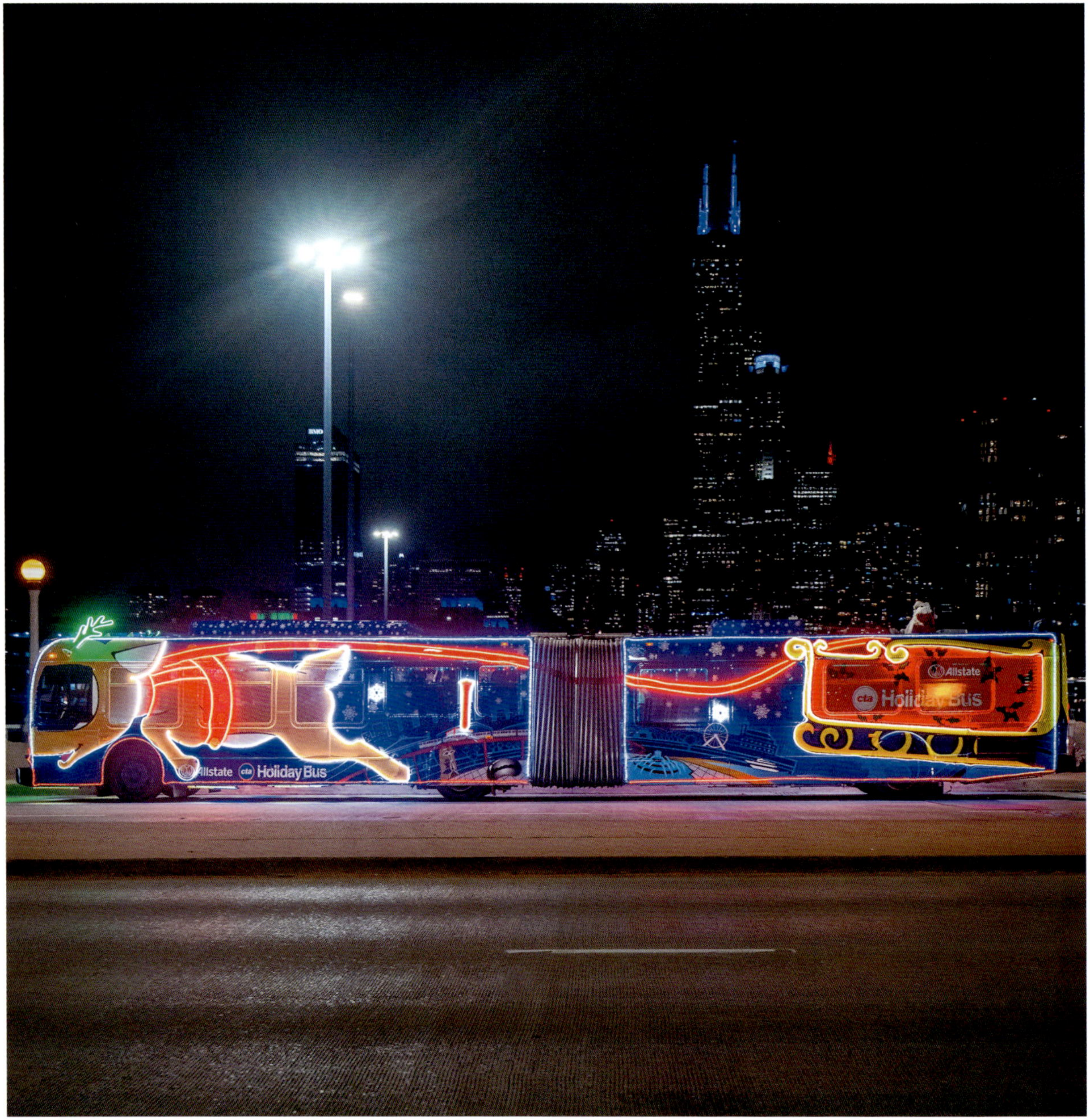

CTA Holiday Bus on Roosevelt Road

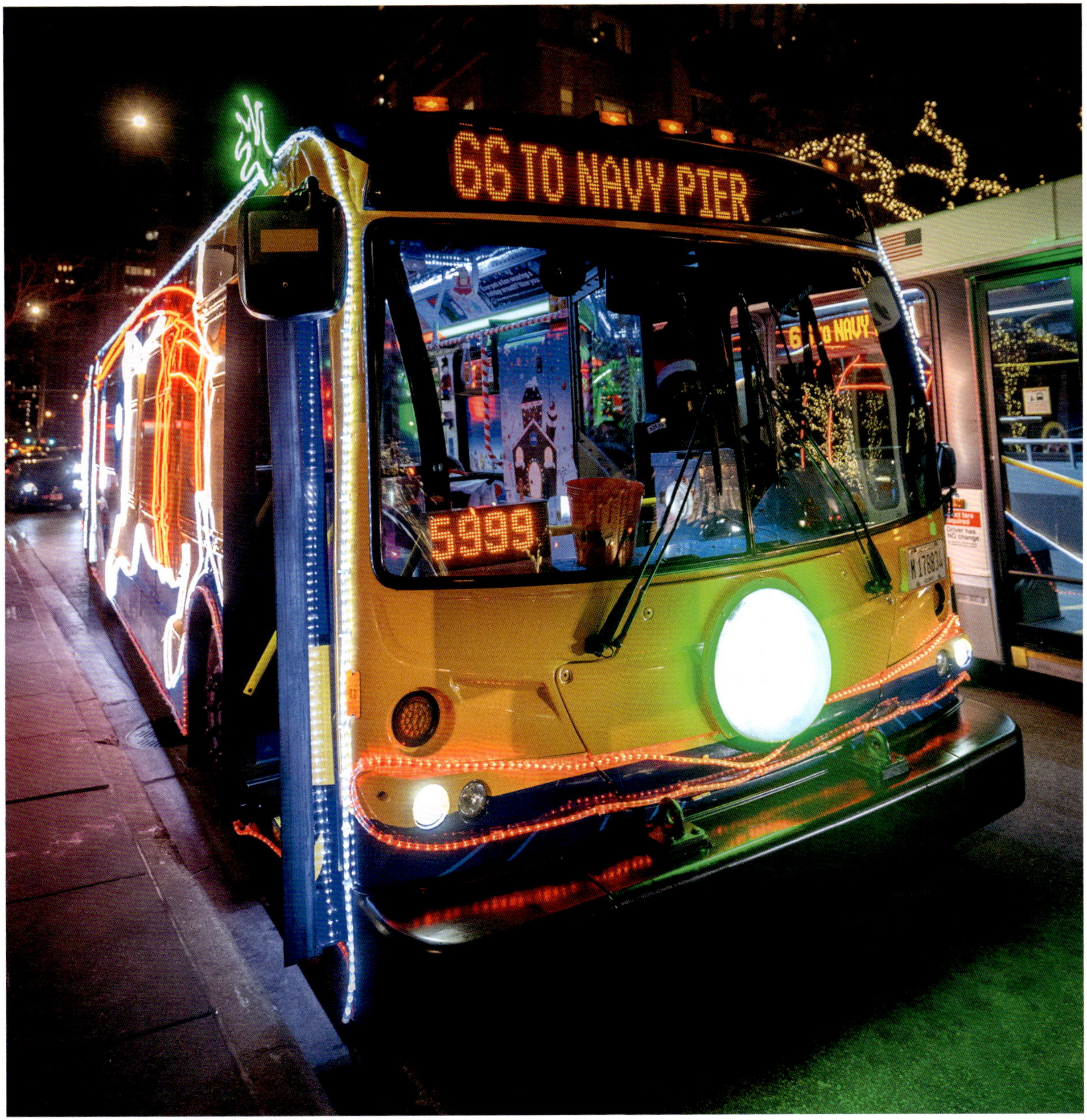

CTA Holiday Bus on West Chicago Avenue

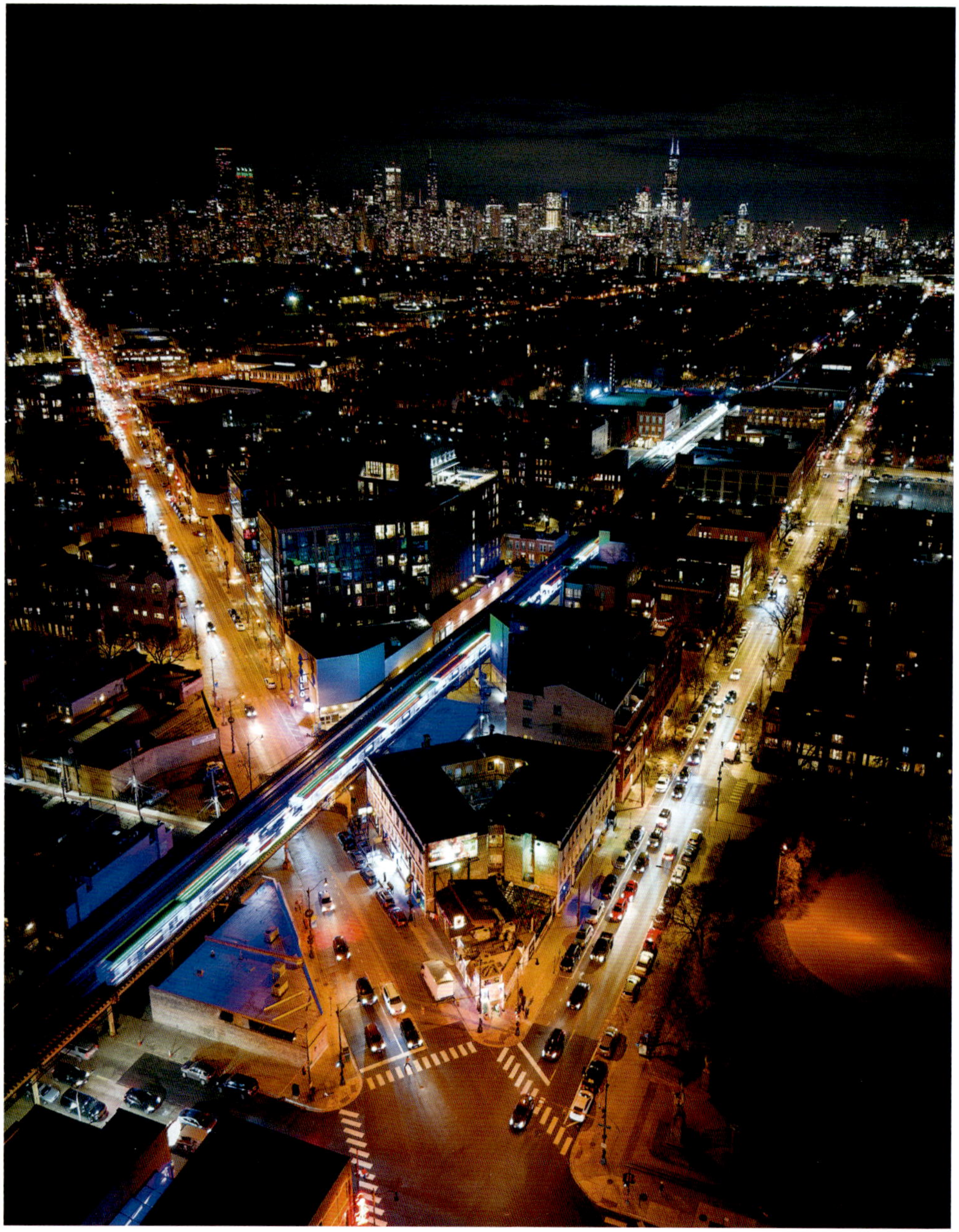

ABOVE: Over North Sheffield Avenue and West Wrightwood Avenue **RIGHT:** Above East 18th Street and South State Street

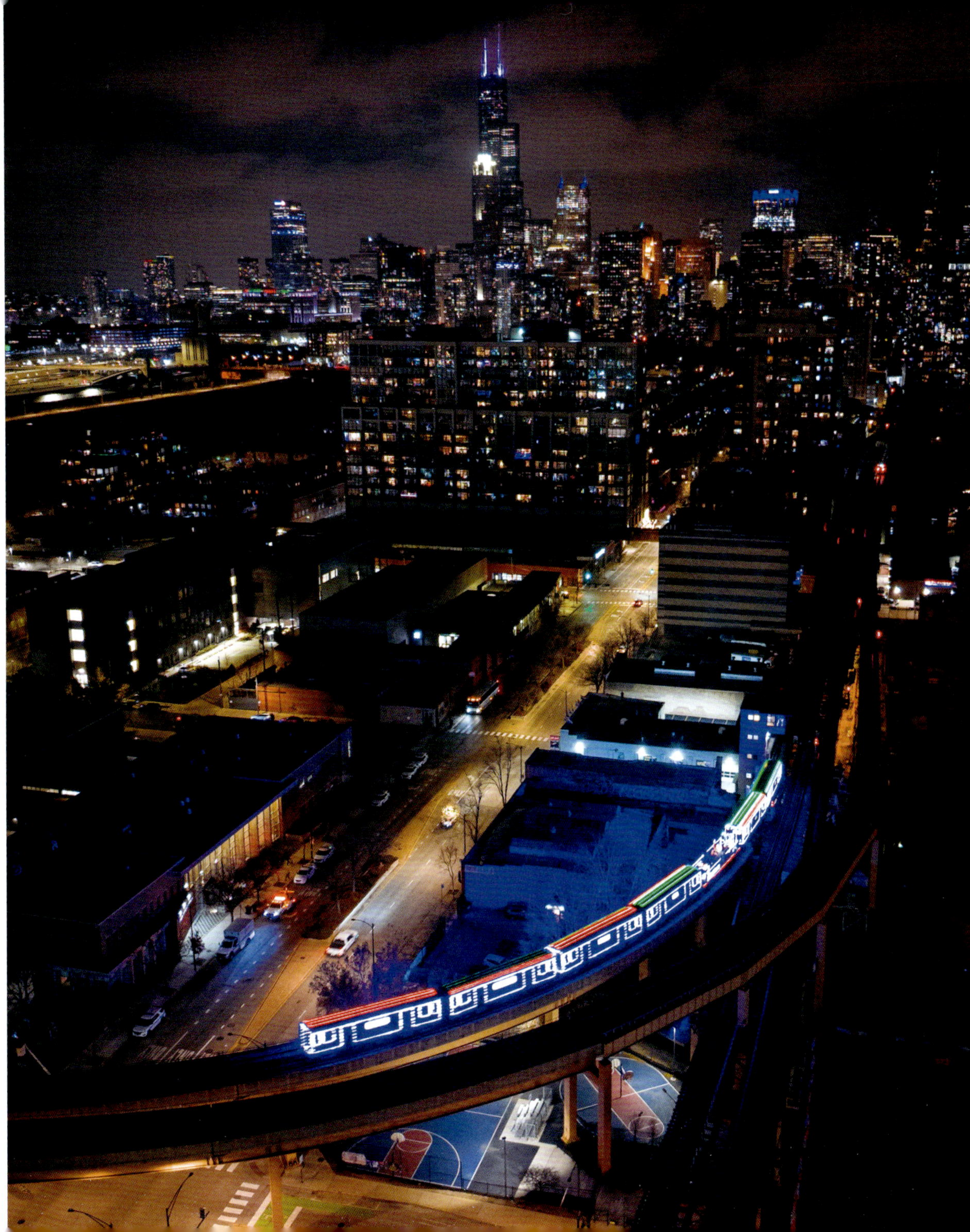

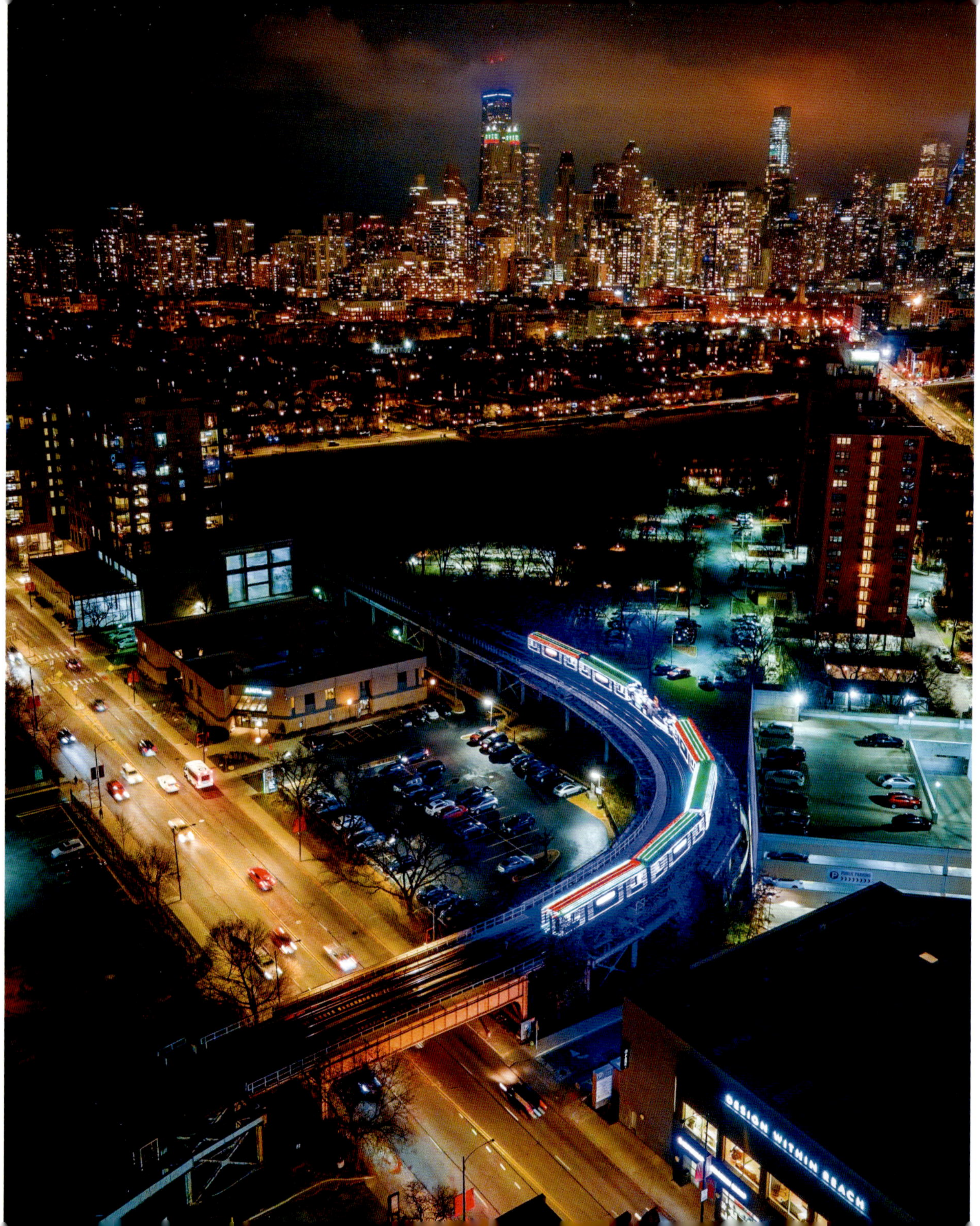
DESIGN WITHIN REACH

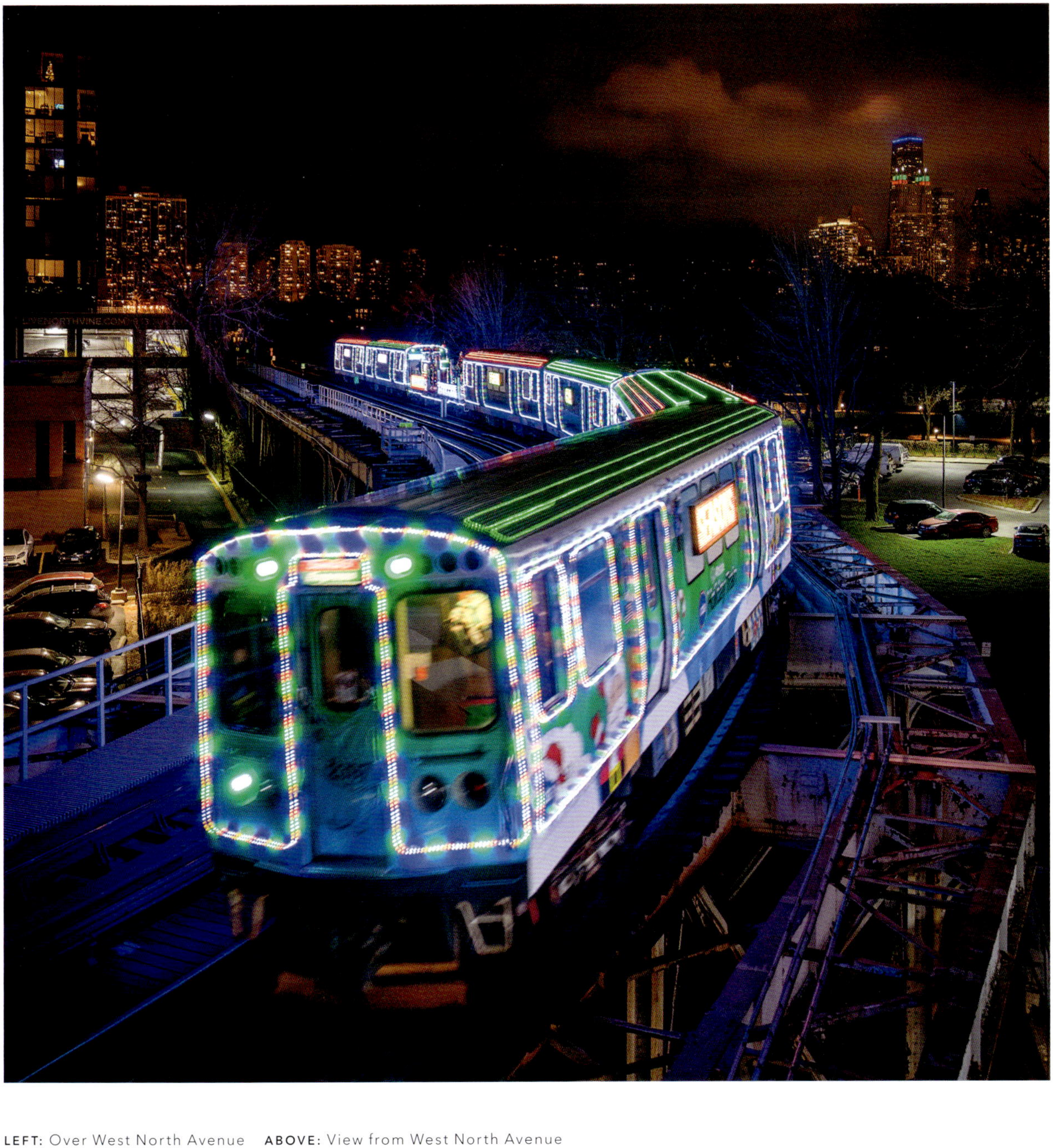

LEFT: Over West North Avenue **ABOVE:** View from West North Avenue

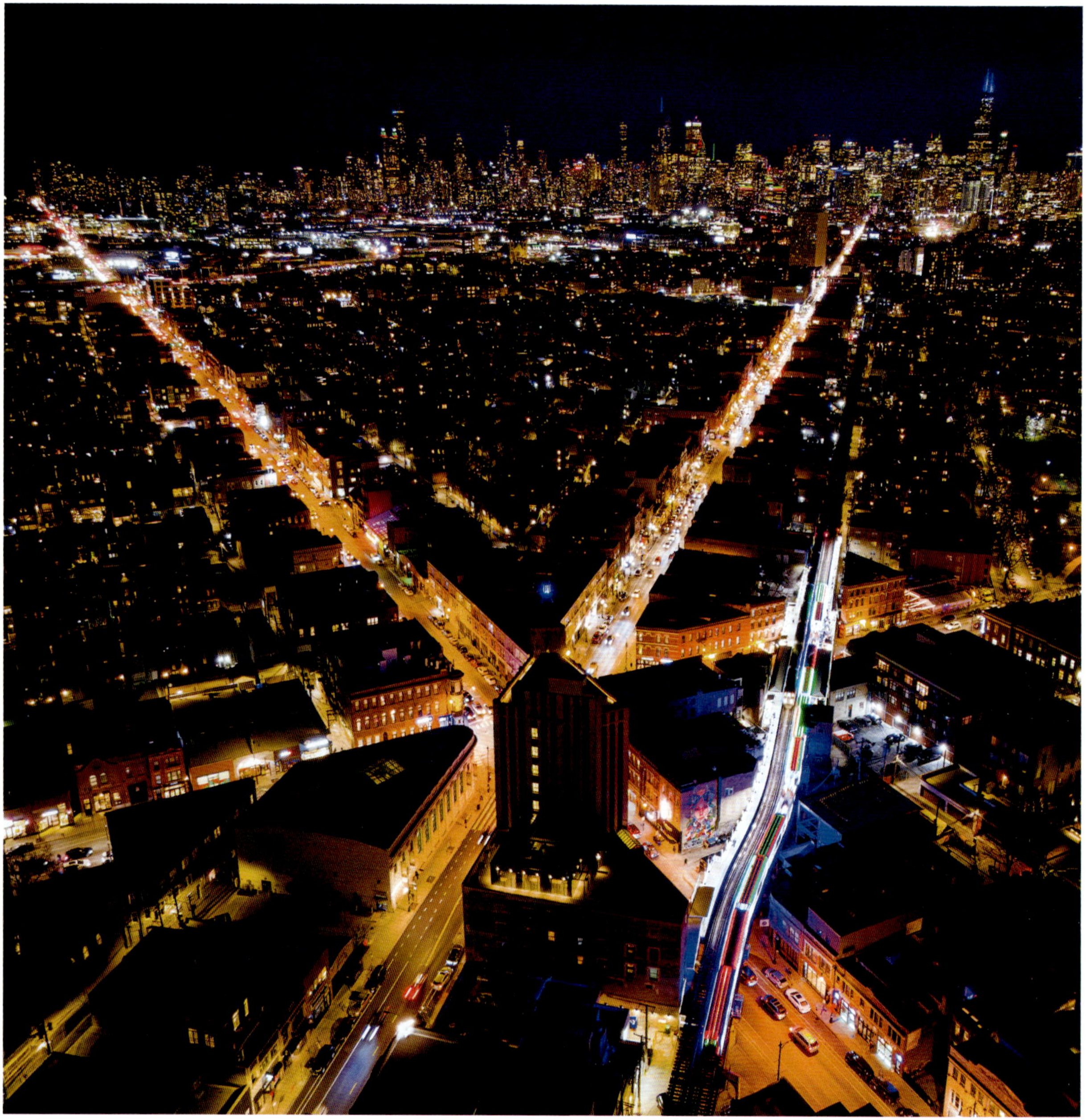

Above Wicker Park

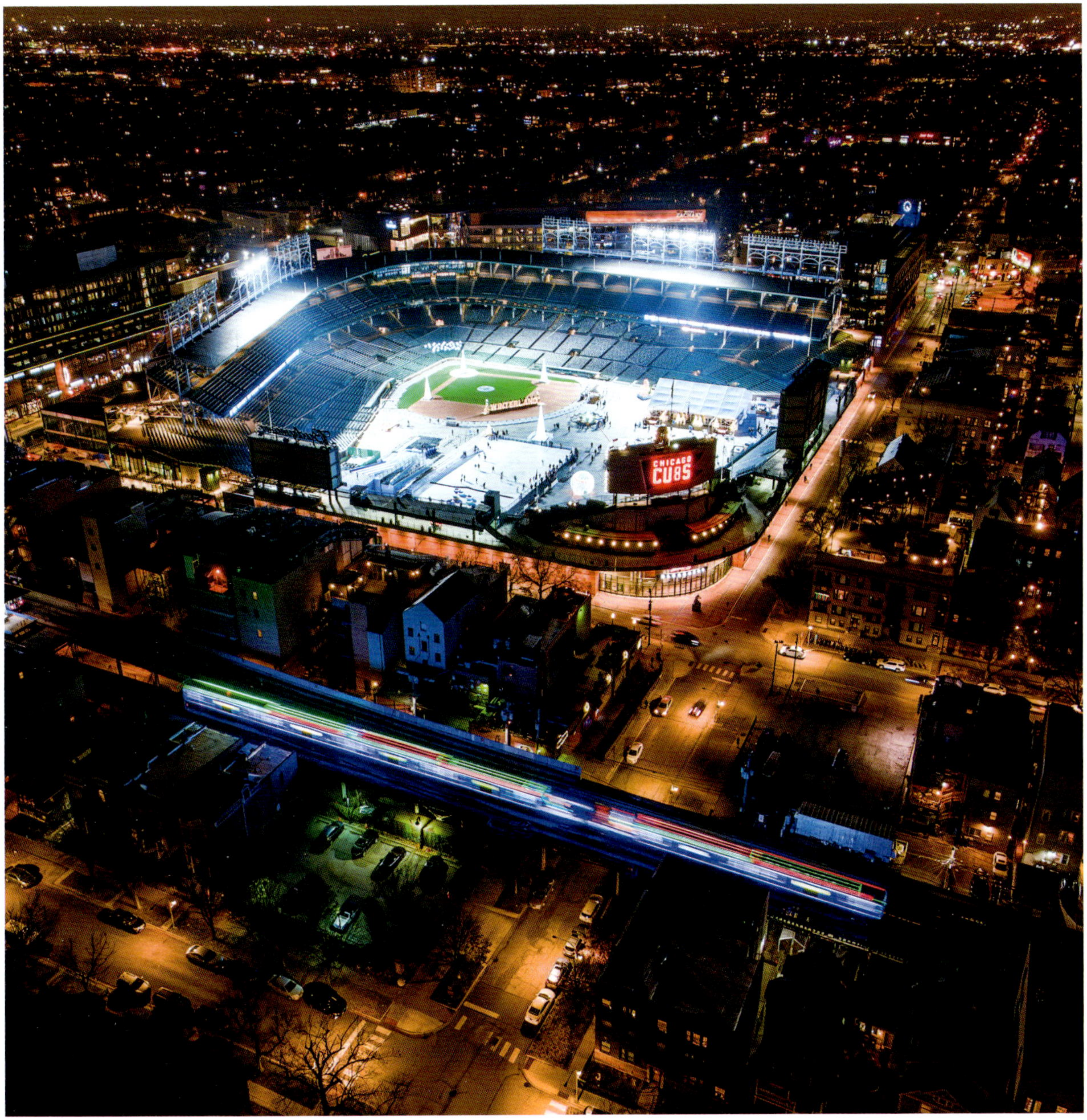

Above Wrigley Field and the Addison station

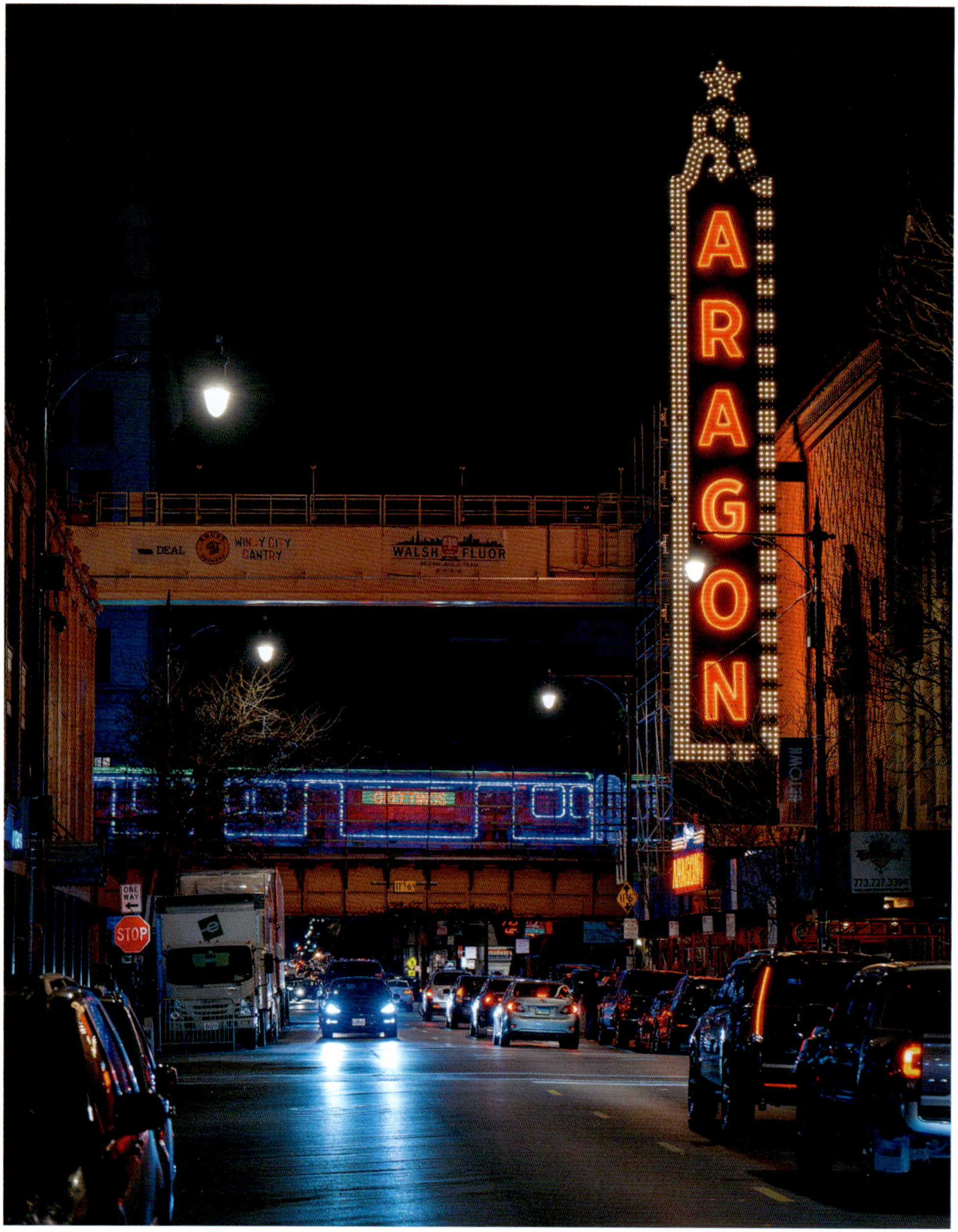

ABOVE: Looking down West Lawrence Avenue **RIGHT:** Looking down West Waveland Avenue

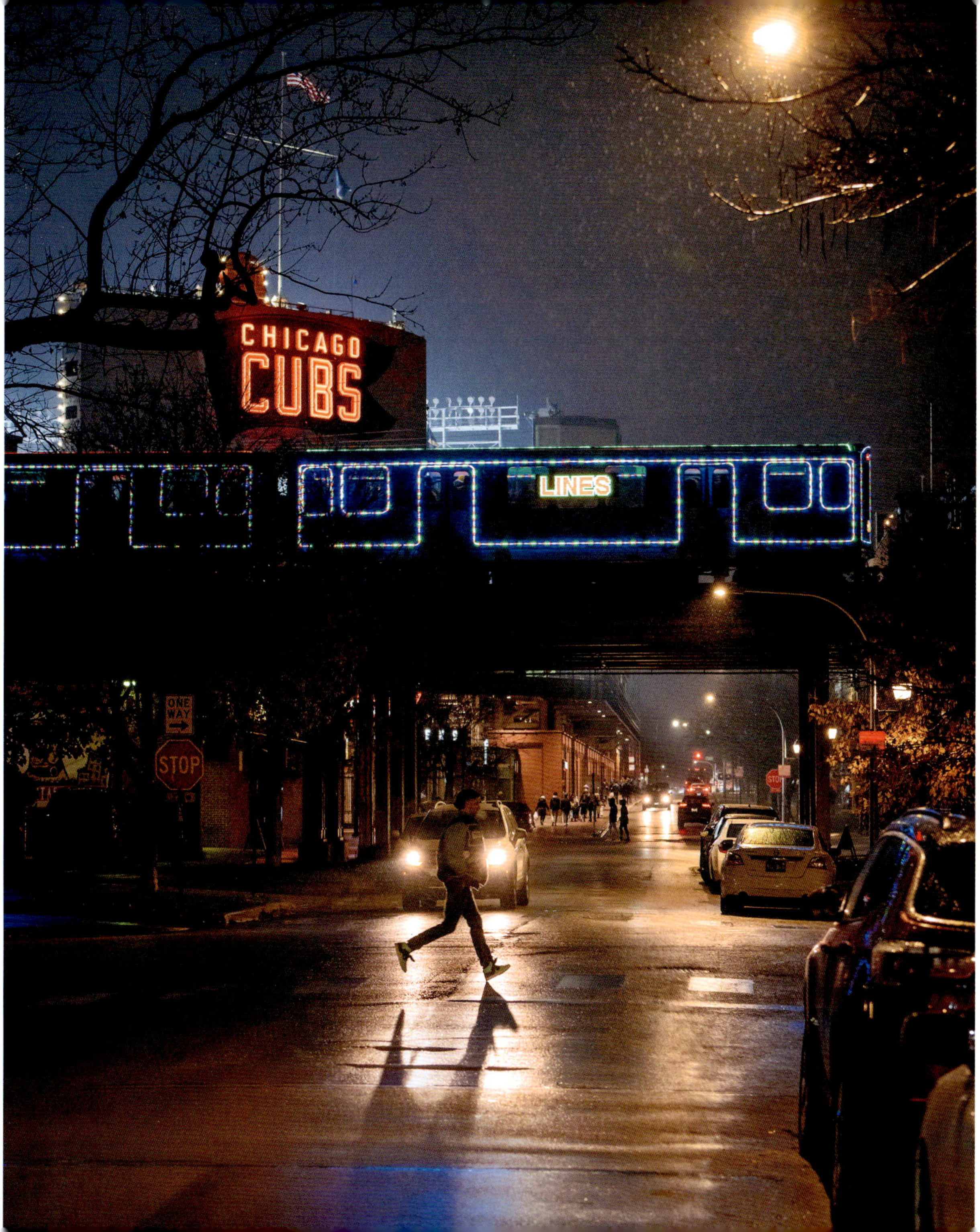
CHICAGO
CUBS
LINES
ONE WAY
STOP

Besides spreading joy, the Holiday Train is used to deliver food baskets to various charitable agencies throughout the city.

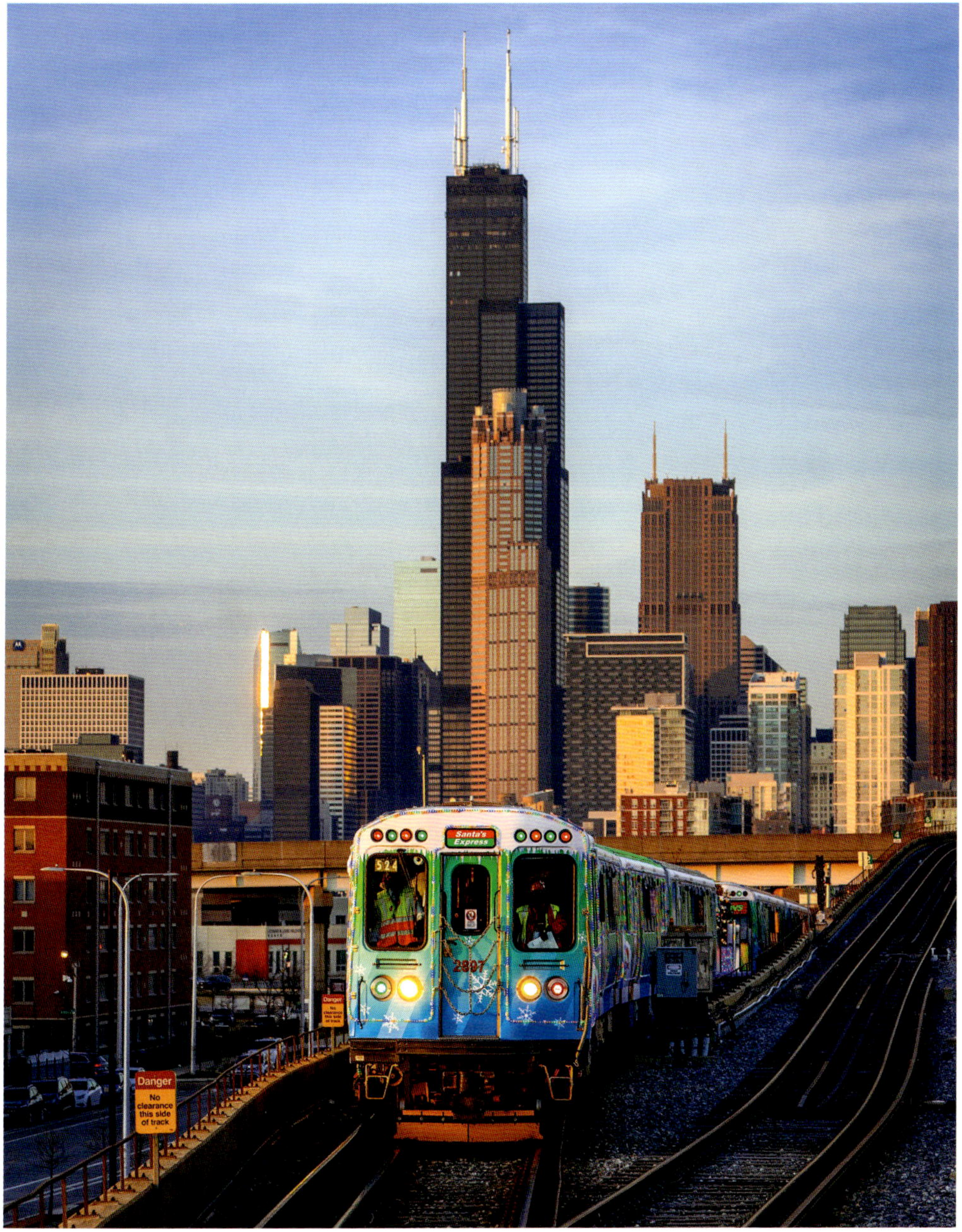

Skyline view from Chinatown station

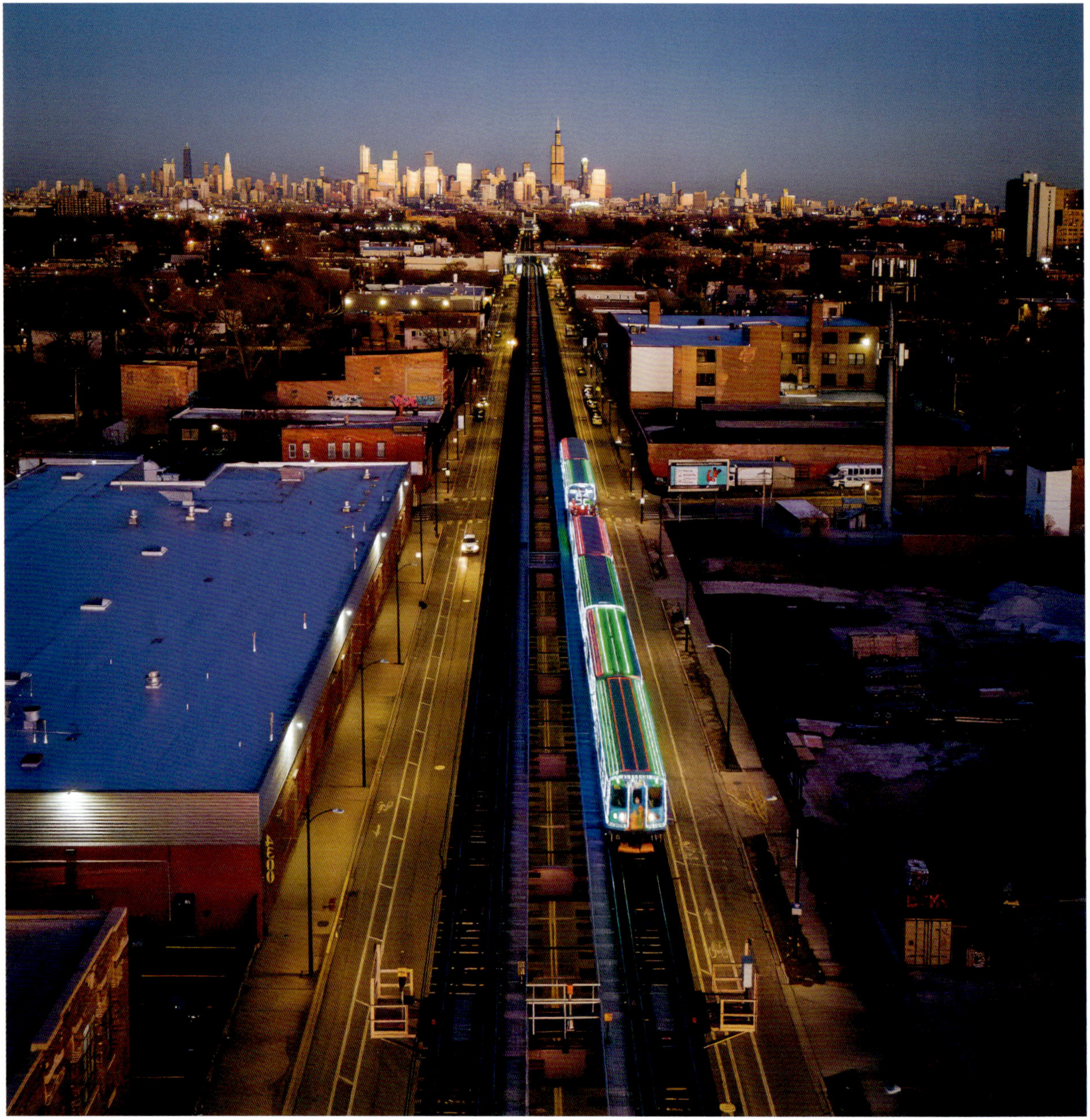

ABOVE: Skyline view from the Cicero station **RIGHT:** View of West Lake Street from the Cicero station

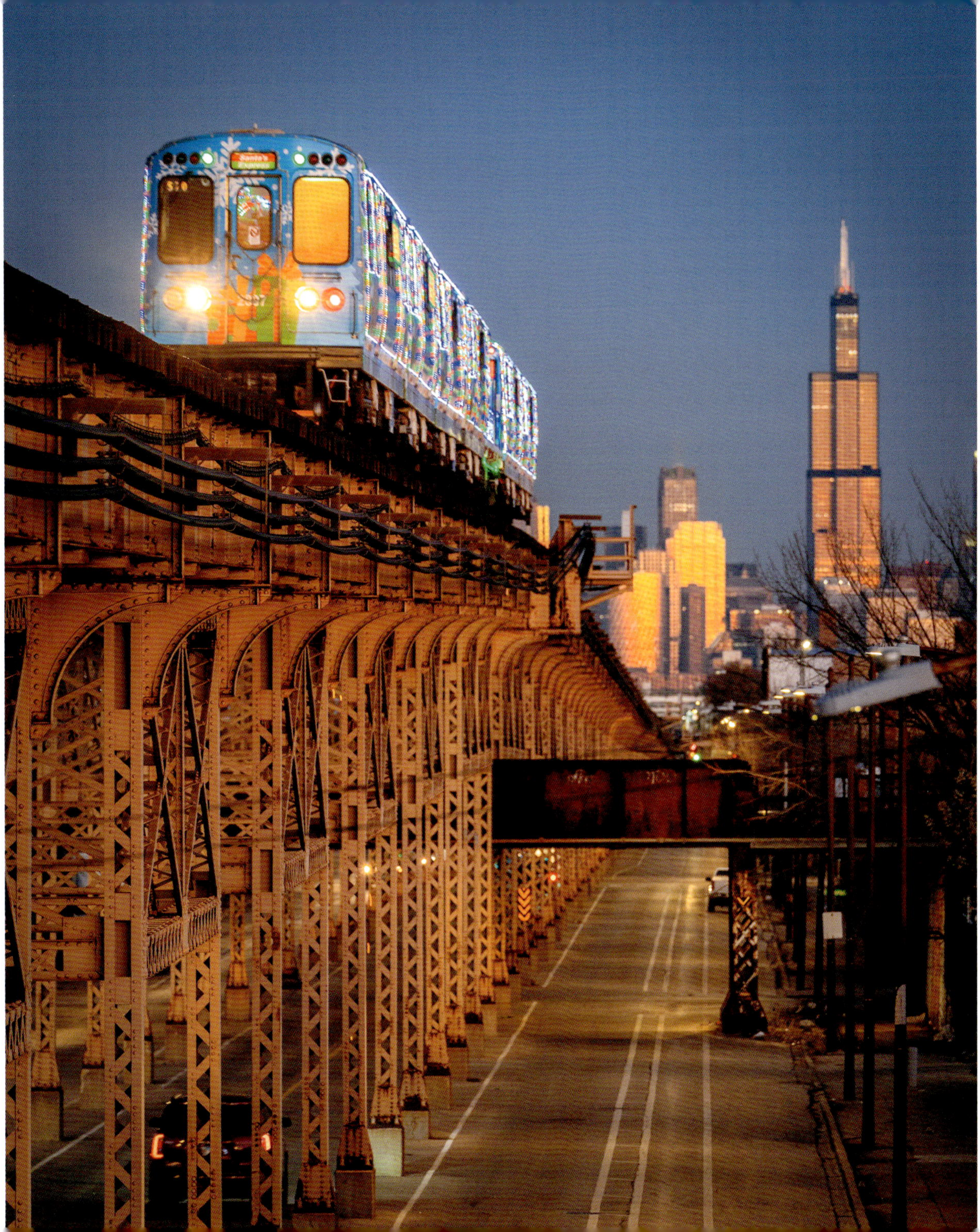

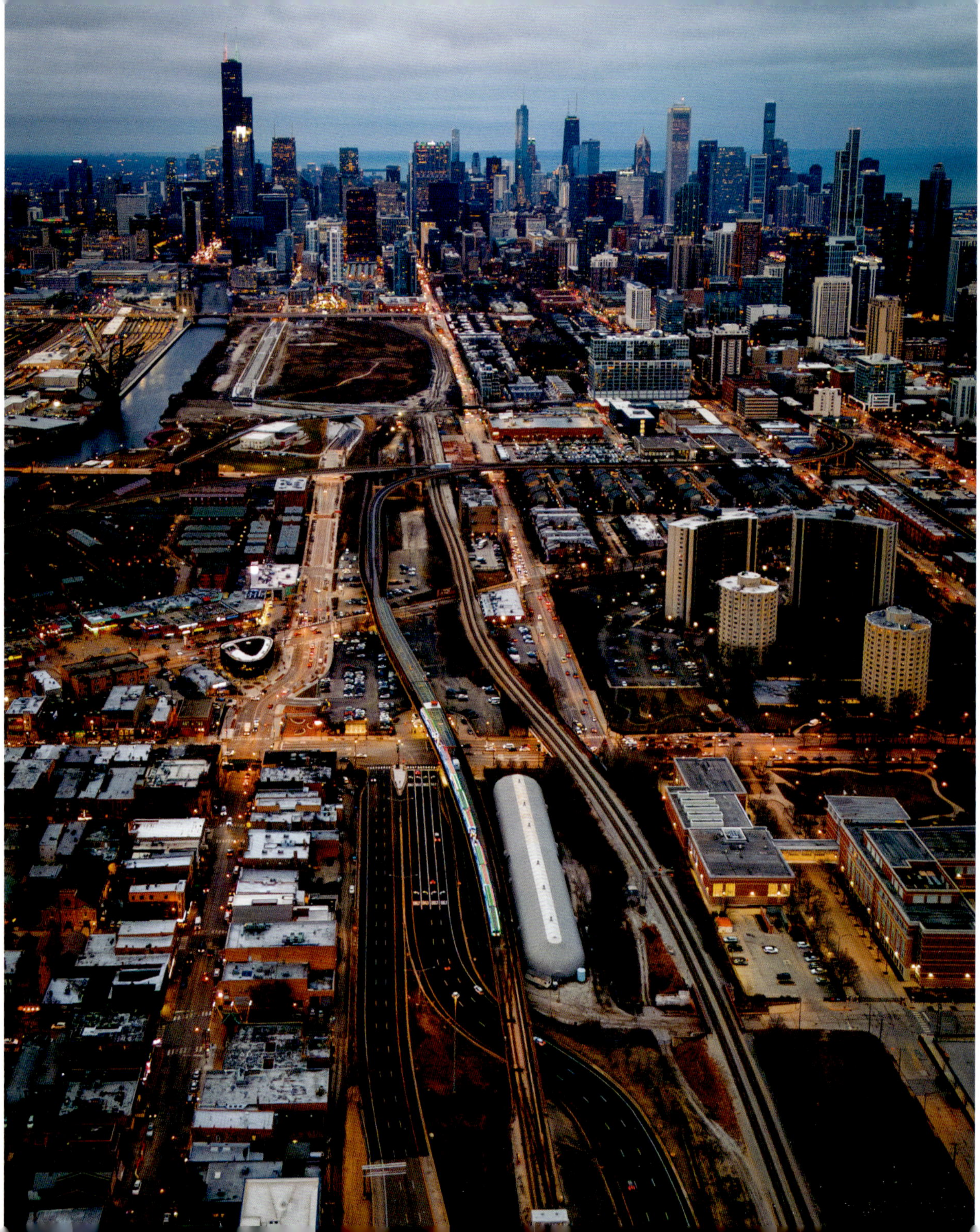

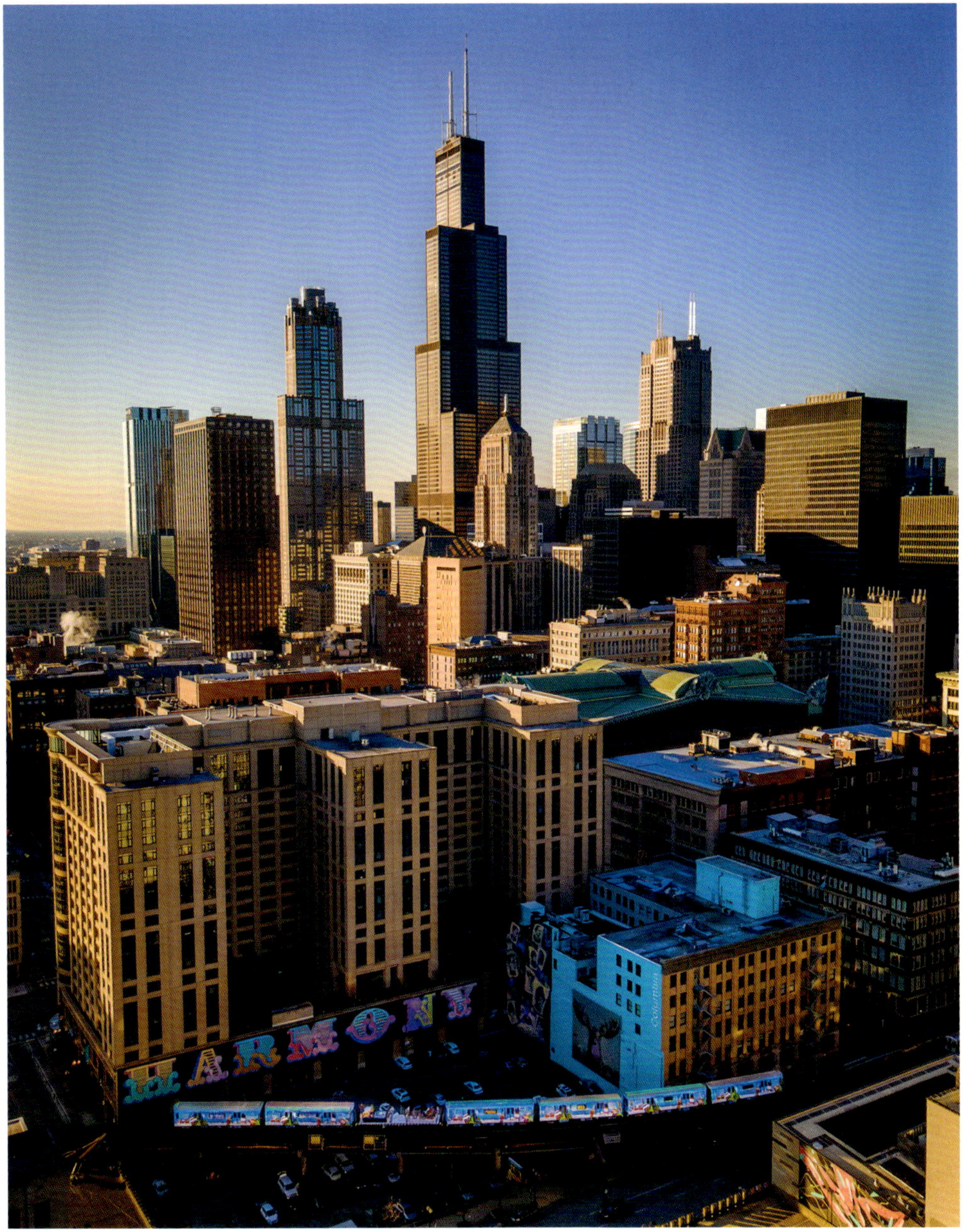

LEFT: Above Chinatown **ABOVE:** Skyline view from South Wabash Avenue

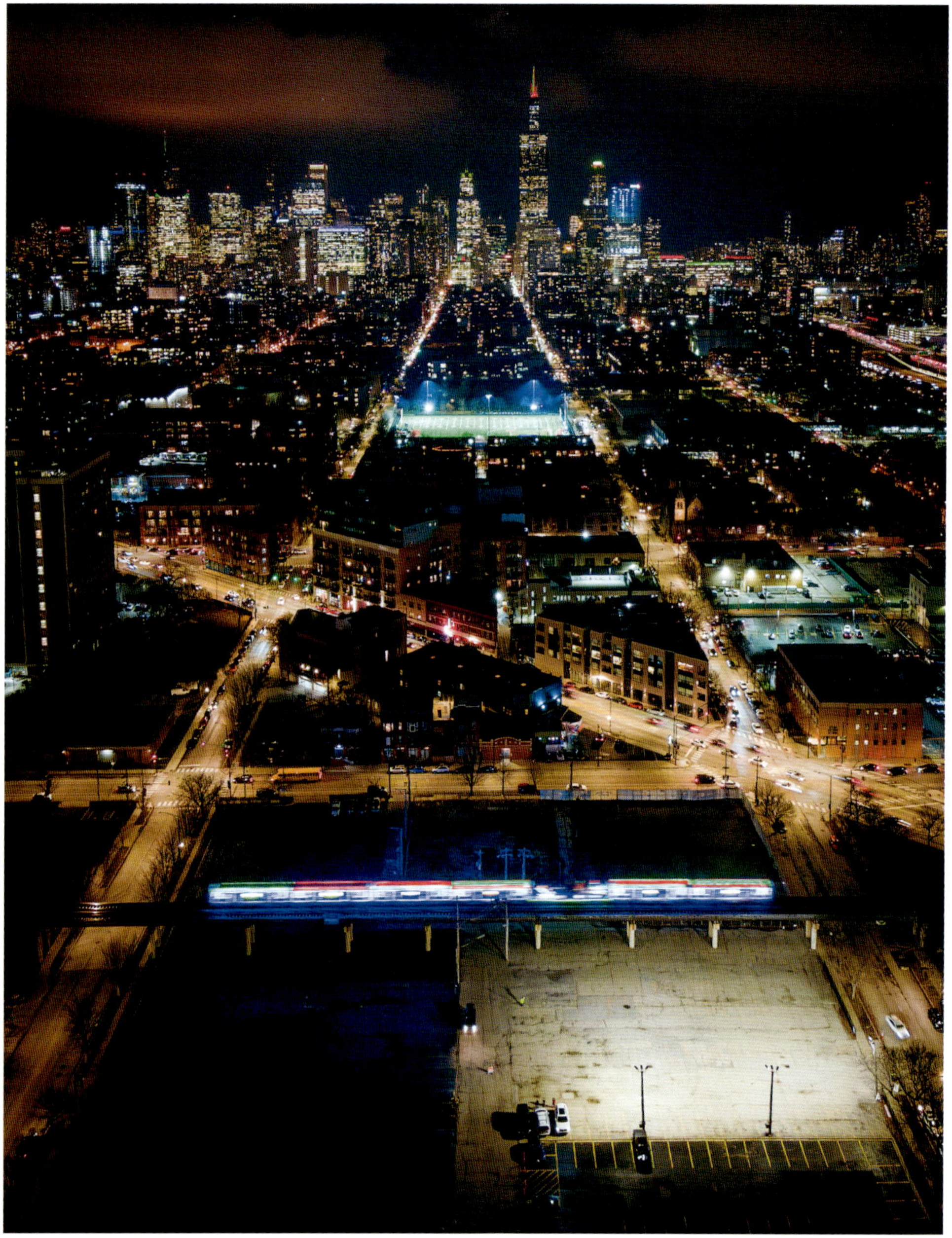

ABOVE: Looking down West Monroe Street and West Adams Street **RIGHT:** Looking down North Broadway Avenue

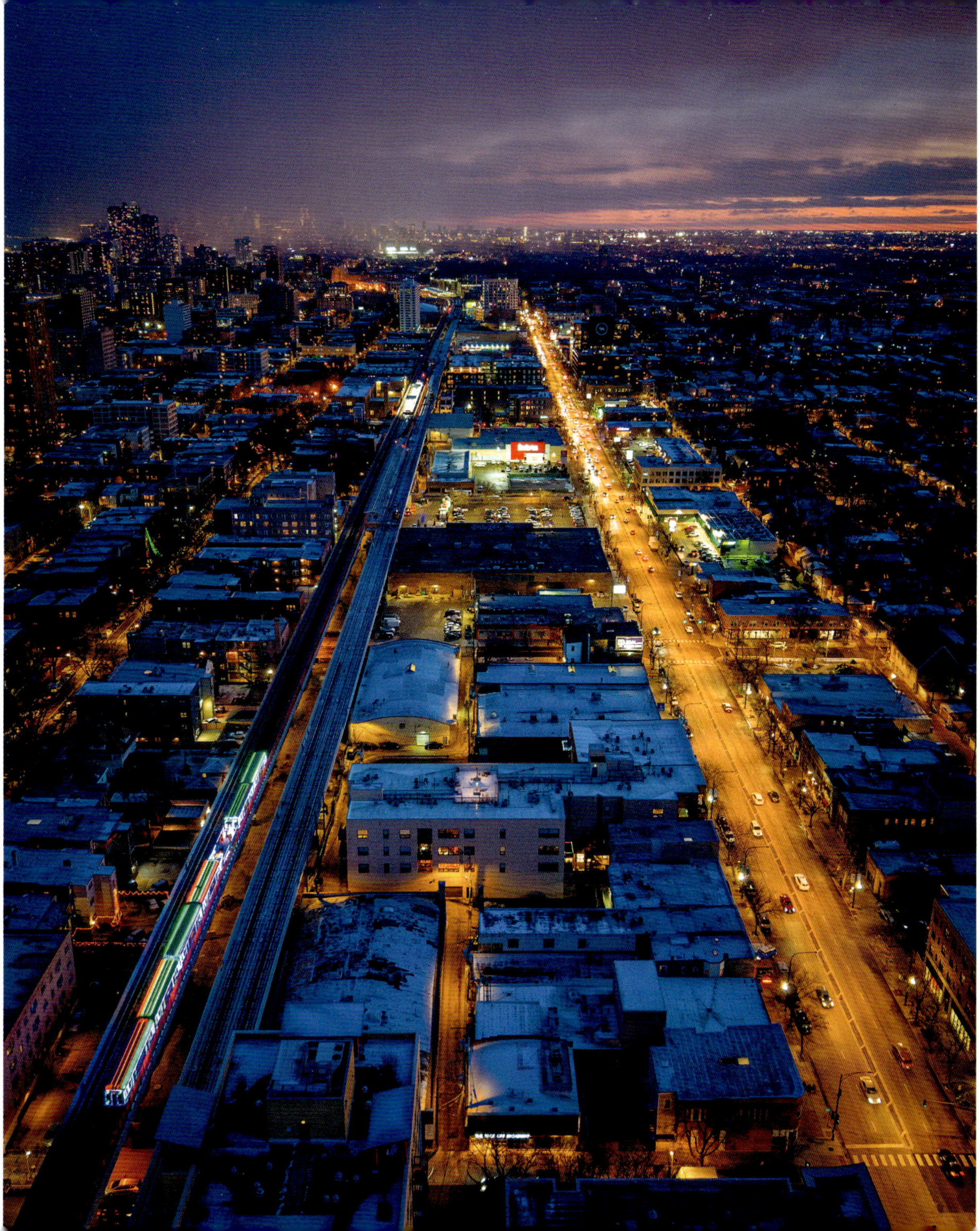

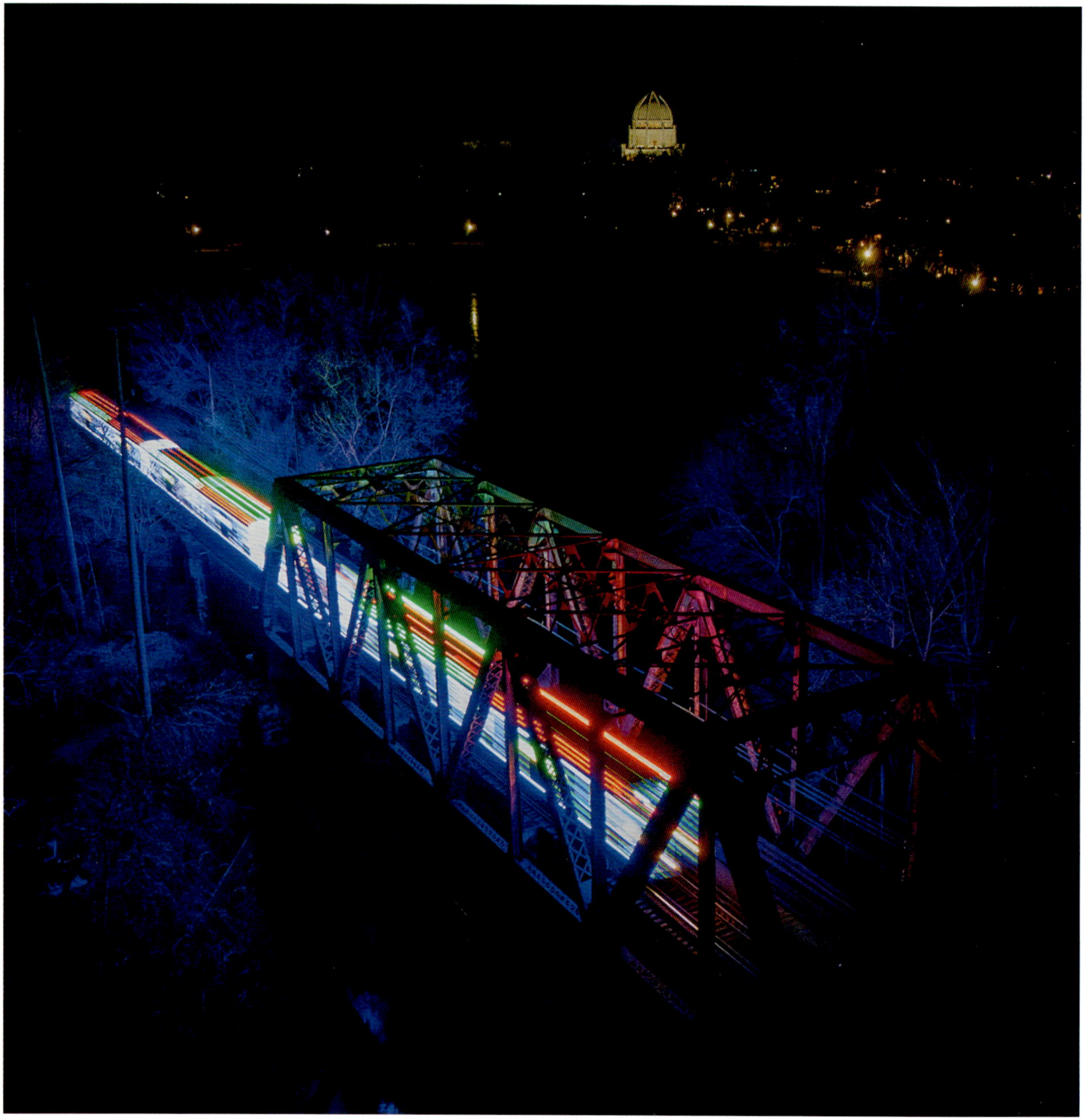

ABOVE: View of the Bahá'i' House of Worship from Evanston **RIGHT:** Skyline view from Morgan station

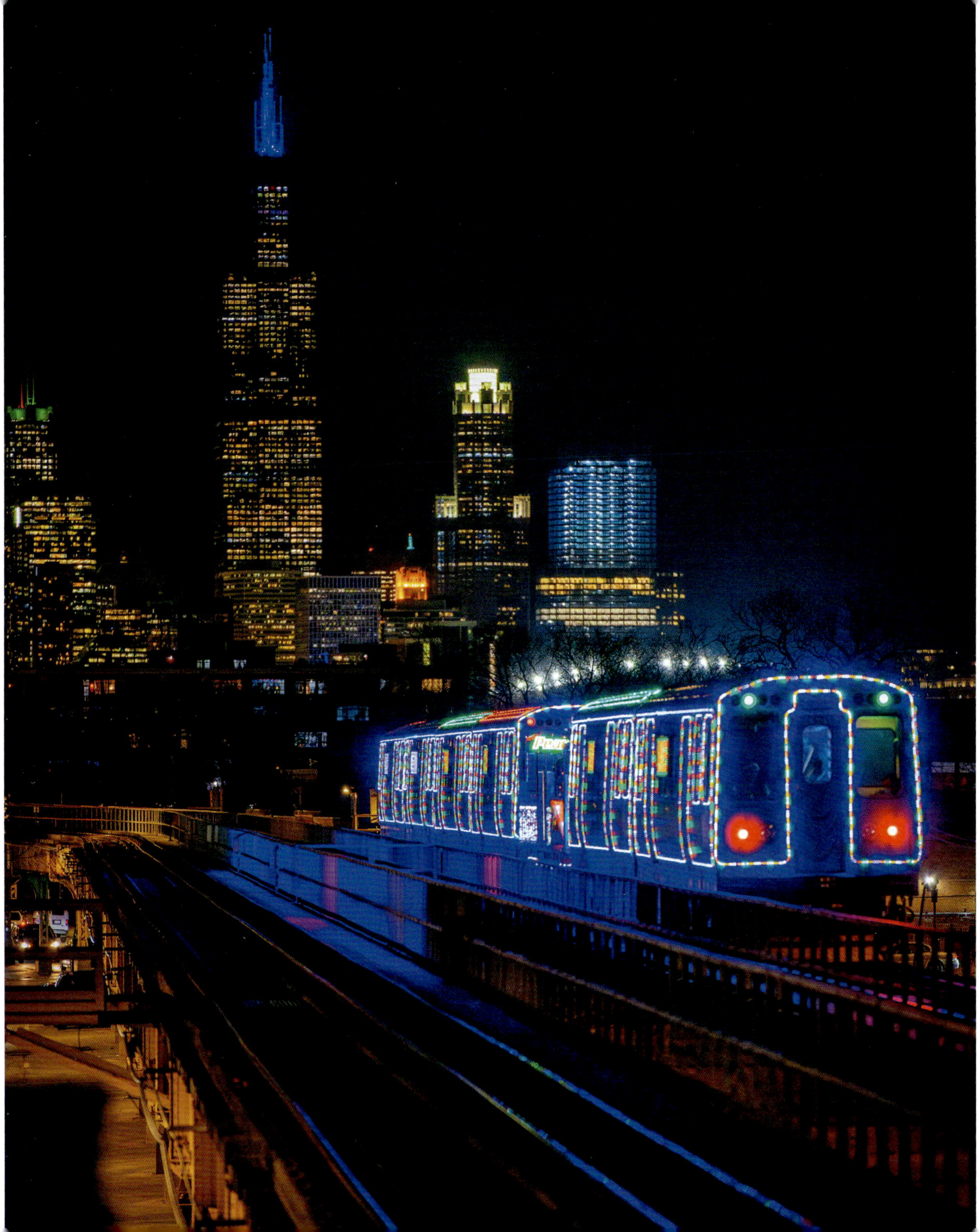

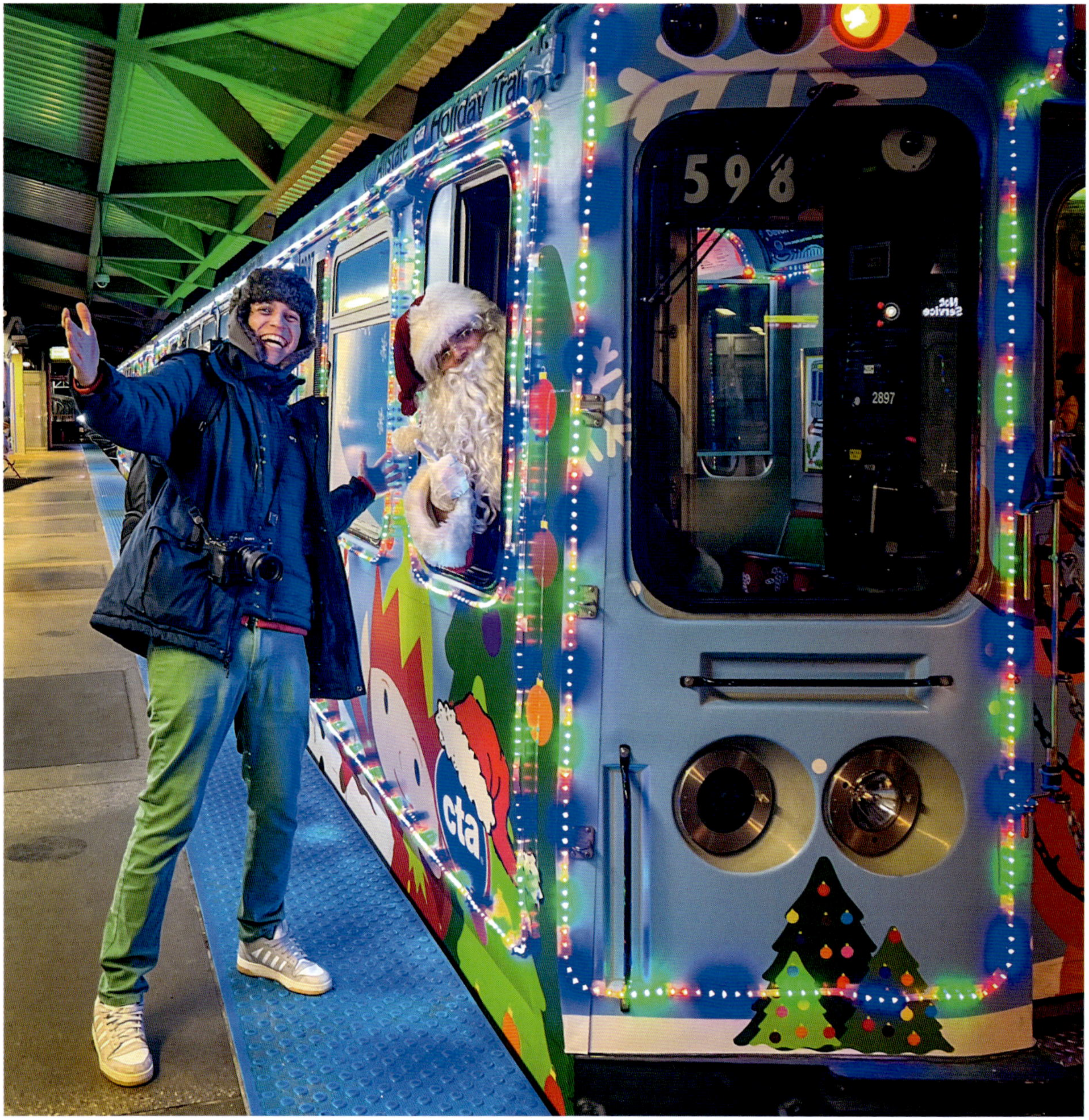
598
2897
cta

ABOUT THE

ARTIST

Daniel Moreno, a photographer from Venezuela now based in Chicago, has been fascinated by film and the audiovisual medium since an early age. This passion naturally led him to discover his love for photography. Captivated by freezing moments in time and finding beauty in everyday surroundings, he believes that life itself is art and the camera serves as a tool to capture those ordinary yet extraordinary moments. Always in pursuit of the perfect shot, Daniel constantly follows the sun and the moon, seeking out urban landscapes and symmetry within the ever-changing cityscape of Chicago. This vibrant city has offered him the opportunity to explore a multitude of photography styles, from ground-level perspectives to capturing the sky, enriching his artistic journey.

LCCN: 2025935447
ISBN: 978-1-951963-42-2

Printed and bound in China
First printing, 2025

Trope Publishing Co.

The photographs from *Chicago's Holiday Train* are available for purchase. For inquiries, email the gallery at info@trope.com

+ INFORMATION:
For additional information on our books and prints, visit trope.com

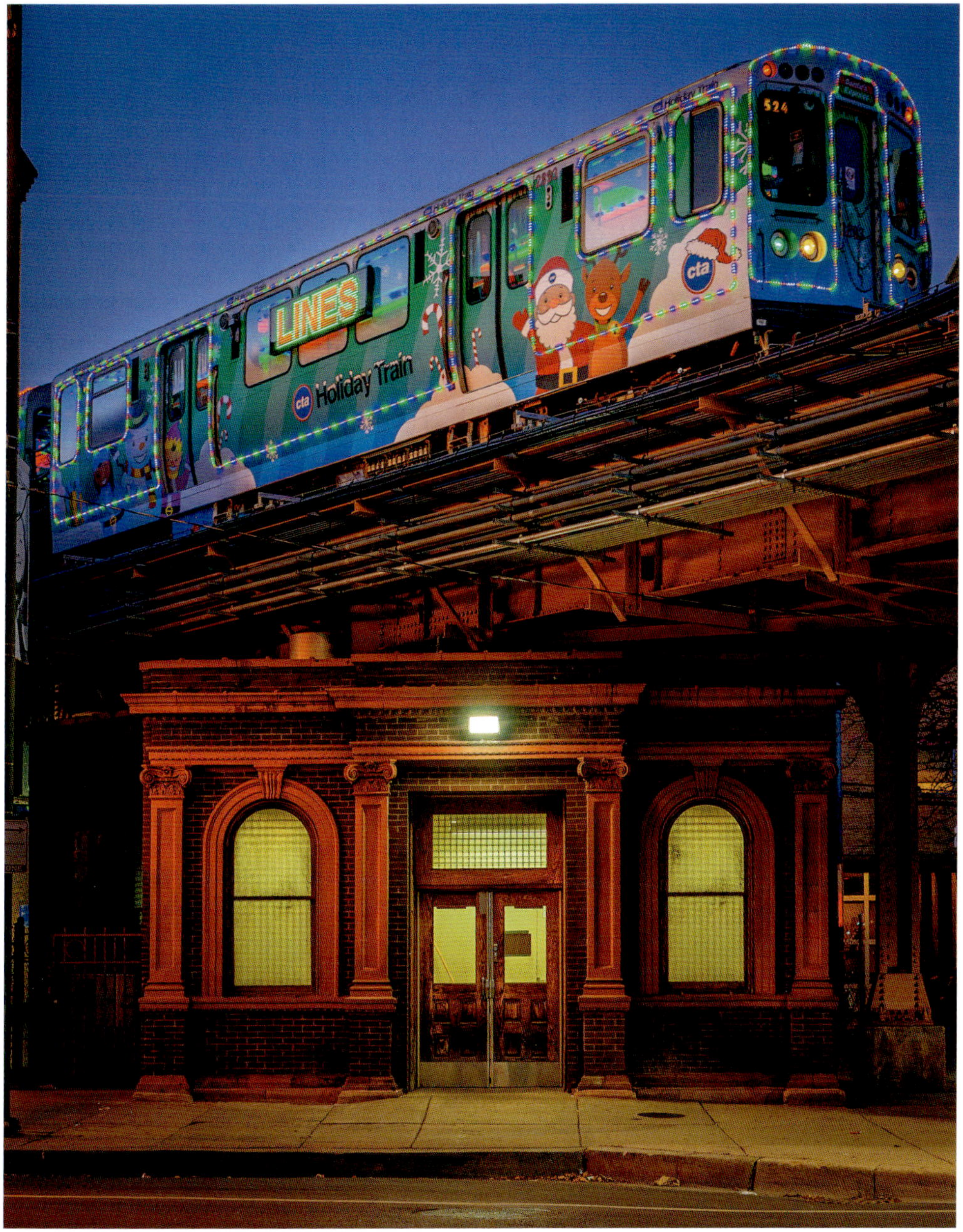
LINES
cta Holiday Train
524

TROPE
PUBLISHING
Co.

Red Line
Green Line

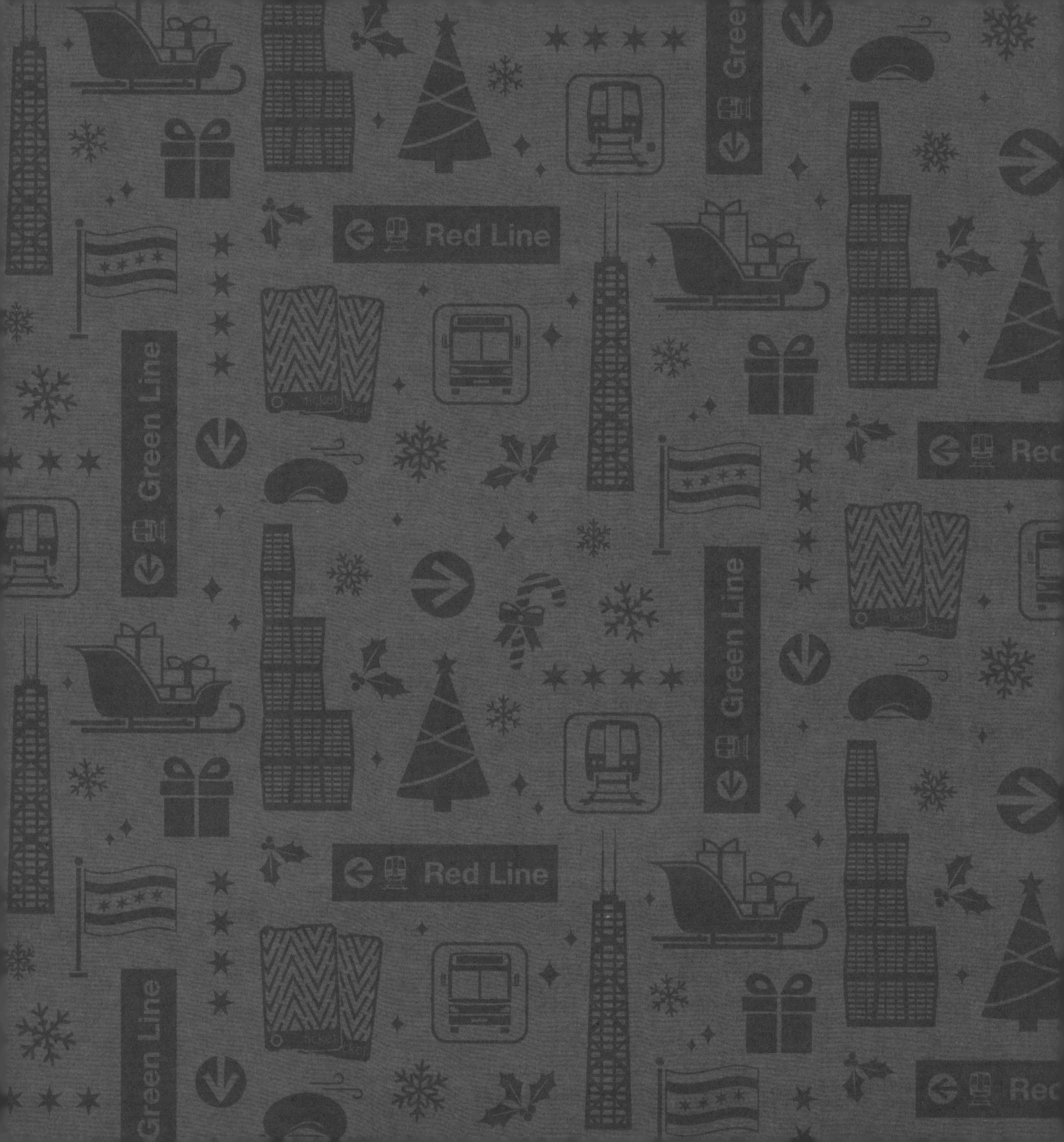

Red Line
Green Line
Green Line
Red Line
Green Line
Red Line
Green Line
Red Line